P9-DEV-778

1. *Godetia vinosa* — 2. *Anothera sinuata* — 3. *Godetia rubicunda* — 4. *Godetia Lepida* —
5. *Godetia tenuifloa* — 6. *Godetia cheiranthifolia* — 7. *Anothera tetraptera* — 8. *Godetia rosea alba* —
9. *Anothera Drummondii* — 10. *Godetia Romanzovii* — 11. *Anothera concinna*.

Susan Erling-Tyrell
The White House,
4775 Pilot House Road,
Tiddlycove,
West Vancouver, B.C.

Tel: 926-9555   January, 1982.

Flower Arranging

a practical guide
to arranging
fresh and dried
flowers

by Helen Chase

Flower Arranging

TREASURY PRESS

First published by Octopus Books Limited
This edition published by Treasury Press
59 Grosvenor Street
London W1

© 1975 Octopus Books Limited

ISBN 0 907407 08 0

Printed in Hong Kong

Contents

Flowers from the Florist

September in the flower shop. Bunches of marigolds, zinnias, dahlias, China asters, snapdragons, fresh strawflowers, cornflowers and daisies still abound, but the tide of chrysanthemums is beginning to flood in. Roses, carnations and the more delicate flowers are stored in ice boxes.

Where does a flower arrangement begin? Does it start with the choice of the flowers, or of the container, or are both of these chosen to suit the needs of a particular spot in your home? It can start at any of these points. If you are in your garden or at the florist's and suddenly find you cannot resist a mass of crisp daisies or a single stalk of rubrum lilies, you return to the house with them to find the right container and background. Or you may want to use a particular table setting or container, and set out to find flowers with certain ideas about their colour and size already in mind. No matter what the genesis of the arrangement, flowers, container or background, the end result should be a pleasing relationship between all three.

Background may seem to be the most rigid of the elements. The colour schemes in the rooms of your home are more or less set. You cannot redecorate for every dinner party or change of season. Remember, though, that flowers are live, natural things and have an unexpected adaptability. A room decorated in shades of rose and green would be ruined if a chair upholstered in yellow were added, but it might gain new warmth and charm from a bowl of daffodils set on a table attracting and reflecting the early spring sunshine.

You may cling to a few favourite containers which look right in certain spots in your home and in which flowers always seem easy to arrange. But even if the background and the container are decided upon first, it is the flowers which bring an arrangement to life and

choosing them is one of the pleasures of arranging. I always had trouble understanding a woman I knew who ordered two bunches of white spray-type chrysanthemums from her florist every two weeks. She did this all year round, in May as well as October. I suppose she was avoiding the inelegance of artificial flowers while getting the most for her money: no cut flower lasts better than the chrysanthemum. But what possible fun can she have had from her flowers? I suppose the answer is that she expected none.

Choosing flowers is a treat. The first thrill is seeing the whole range of flowers laid out before you in your garden or at the florist's shop and browsing among them like a butterfly soaking up the colours and scents. The next pleasure is making up your mind which is the greatest current treasure to be brought into your home for more lengthy enjoyment. Your choice will be dictated largely by your personal likes and dislikes and what you think goes well in your home, but your satisfaction with the choice will be greater if you make it forearmed with a little knowledge.

Knowing what to cut when in the garden, and what is really a good buy at the florist's, is not really terribly complicated, but it is surprising how few people, even flower lovers, seem to know much about it. It is worthwhile to take the time to learn a few basics and then to practise using your senses in applying them.

This first chapter is devoted to buying flowers. The gardener who brings

flowers he has raised into the house has a greater joy, of course, than anyone who simply buys them possibly could have. However, the exigencies of season, available growing space and time are likely to drive even the most dedicated gardener into a florist's once in a while, and many people are completely dependent on florists for all their flowers.

An essential step is to choose a good florist. There should be one in your vicinity who offers good quality flowers in a wide variety. He should also be able to provide an efficient service when you need to have flowers sent. A busy florist is frequently, although not invariably, a good one. A rapid turnover of stock lessens the chances of flowers stagnating in a corner and of a florist being tempted to sell them to you to 'get his money back'.

Never be afraid to go into a shop in an elegant location and ask a few prices. You may be surprised. The rich are often just as careful of their money, or more so, than the rest of us. Ask the prices of a few staple items: a bunch of daisies, pompon chrysanthemums, a dozen carnations, snapdragons or miniature roses. A little comparison shopping should tell you if the prices are competitive.

You must expect to pay more for the rarer flowers stocked by a good florist. After all, he does. A mediocre florist will probably not even bother with them because of the risk involved.

You might also ask what a florist's policy is about splitting dozens and bunches. It varies. Normally, flowers

which are sold by the dozen can also be bought by the 'piece'. In other words, just as you can buy a single red rose (the symbol of love and one of the commonest sales a florist makes), you should be able to buy one or any number you want of carnations, irises, large chrysanthemums, etc. Some florists will, and some will not, split flowers which come in bunches. Being able to buy single pieces and half bunches is handy, either when your budget is tight and you have to content yourself with filling a bud vase, or when you are making a mixed bouquet and want to include only a few of each type of flower.

Florists are very hard-working men and women. Their days are long and so are their weeks. Because of the perishability of the commodity they sell, there is a high rate of bankruptcy in the trade, although it is interesting to note that the rate does not seem to increase during periods of general depression. Perhaps more people than one would imagine

subscribe to the old Dutch saying: 'If you have but two guilder in your pocket, buy a loaf of bread with one, and with the other buy a hyacinth for your soul.'

Like any other group, florists come in varying shades of honesty. Their universal aim is to stay in business and make a reasonable profit. To do this they have to move as much of their merchandise as they can in a relatively short period of time, and they also have to keep a good body of satisfied customers coming back on a regular basis. It can be a fine line to tread on occasion, but a reputable, established florist would not knowingly 'stick' a good customer with flowers in poor condition.

The best insurance for buying fresh flowers, then, is to be a good customer at a good florist's shop. A 'good' customer is not necessarily one who spends a great deal of money. Of course, a large account, particularly if it is paid with reasonable promptness, does not diminish a customer's standing in a florist's

eyes, but a person with a modest flower budget can easily qualify as a good customer.

A good customer is one who deals fairly regularly with the same florist (loyalty tends to beget loyalty), who knows what she wants, what she is buying, how to treat it when she gets home, and what to expect of it. Do this with a pleasant attitude and your florist will prove a valuable ally. If you appreciate that his time is valuable, especially in busy seasons, he will probably go out of his way to give you the best advice, to tell you when he has found a 'buy' in the market of flowers which are usually more expensive, and to make sure that you get exactly what you want. If you warn him a day or two in advance, he can often order you special flowers.

Florists rarely mind answering reasonable questions; it is part of their job and if they are not rushed and the customer is pleasant they often enjoy talking about flowers. However, there is one question I am afraid it is a waste of breath asking: 'Are you sure these flowers are perfectly fresh?' or, worse still, 'Did you get these in this morning?' They hear these questions so often that they develop a kind of occupational deafness and respond automatically, 'Yes, madam, they couldn't be fresher', with a smile of wonderful sincerity. This answer is not gravely dishonest even when it is not the strict truth. It is simply the shortest way to tell the customer what he or she really wants to know: that the flowers in question are in good condition and will last as long in the home as flowers of their type can be expected to last. (There is a wide difference in the life span of a cut daffodil and a cut chrysanthemum.) Of course, a florist will try to steer any customer he hopes to see again away from flowers he knows are not going to last in the home. He expects to use at least some of these in funeral pieces, where, having drunk their fill in the shop, they will stand up

Roses and chrysanthemums are two of the most popular florists' flowers. Choose roses with straight stems and some buds which will open later. Chrysanthemums should be crisp and erect on their stems, with fresh green foliage and firm round flower heads.

All flowers should be cut
at a slanting angle with
a sharp knife or scissors.

of colour, form and size which will be pleasing not only in the garden but also in arrangements in the different rooms of your home. If shades of yellow, gold and orange fit in well with your decor, you have a wealth of early and late yellow and orange daffodils, narcissi and tulips to choose from. If the golden tones are not the most flattering ones for your home, you are not stuck with them in spring. Use the wonderfully pure and elegant white and creamy daffodils and narcissi combined with pink, rose and purple-black tulips. Darwins, the good old standbys for mass planting in the garden, seem to me the least interesting of the tulips for arranging. Try some of the lily-flowered and parrot varieties. They last well and their forms are fascinating.

Nothing pays bigger dividends for the amount of space and time they take in the garden than the tiny spring bulbs; just as the little spots of life they create wake up the garden, miniature arrangements of them wake up the house. Some of them are fragile, others, such as grape hyacinths, last well. Snowdrops wear like iron.

Many flowering shrubs and trees can also be planted in the autumn. Pussy willow, forsythia, dogwood, japonica (flowering quince) and other ornamental fruit trees, lilac, philadelphus, magnolia, rhododendron and hawthorn

all add height and variety of form and feeling to spring arrangements. Looking ahead, snowball bush provides flowers for large summer arrangements and dries beautifully.

As the spring bulbs fade, the perennials begin their reign. With exceptions these are planted in the autumn or early spring. Bearded irises, garden favourites, are not as satisfactory for cut flowers as the Japanese, Siberian and Dutch types. (If you do arrange with the bearded iris, keep the dead heads picked off and do not let the blossoms rest against walls or furniture – they leave a nasty stain.) Peonies are well worth the trouble it may take to get them happily established in the garden. If you do Oriental line arrangements, plant a few tree peonies. Their large single blossoms achieve the perfection of a carved Chinese screen.

Delphiniums are so beautiful in their shades of blue that I can never resist using them even if I do have to dust under the arrangement frequently. The Pacific hybrids shed less than the belladonnas, although the latter, commoner strain produces more flower heads for arranging. Delphiniums, like lupins, foxgloves, eremuri (foxtail lilies) and others are valuable because of their long, spiky shape which gives height and grace to your arrangements. Oriental poppies, border carnations, daisies

and asters are a few among the many round-flowered perennials you can grow.

If your soil is well drained, try some of the summer bulbs: ranunculi, anemones, dahlias and gladioli. The last are not a great favourite of mine; to me they look awkward in the garden and funereal in arrangements, but I cannot deny the spiky, formal shape and the lasting quality for which many arrangers value them. Rubrum lilies in the pink colour range, and Mid-Centuries in the orange, are wonderful in arrangements. So are the small, curly Turk's-cap varieties and the Madonnas. If you have a suitable spot in the garden and a liking for arrangements on a majestic scale, grow some auratum and longiflorum lilies.

No garden should be without a few rose bushes. Garden roses may not have the long, straight stems of commercially grown ones, but they have a quality and a feeling seldom found in florists' roses. You can have them in any colour range except blue and in the subtlest variations of shades to suit you and your home. I like having some floribundas spray types as contrasts to the hybrid teas. Many of the modern floribundas have been so 'improved' by hybridization that the distinction is lost.

As your garden bursts into the full glory of spring and early summer you should be planning ahead for mid-summer and autumn. This is the time to plant annuals and chrysanthemums in shades from white through rose to lavender, and palest yellow through gold to deepest bronze and russet-red. You need not limit yourself to the usual pompon types of chrysanthemum since there are now many hardy varieties which produce tiny button and daisy forms, thread and spoon-shaped petals. Check their flowering times so that you can arrange a steady succession from late summer past hard frost.

Annuals have a rightful place in the garden. If I seem defensive in making such a statement, it is the result of my having known several gardeners (all men, coincidentally) who felt that annuals were not worth bothering with because they had to be replanted every year. However, for the person who is addicted to having flowers in the house and wants a steady supply through the hot summer months they are indispensable. Some of the grandest flowers are perennials but, with some exceptions, their blooming seasons are limited to two or three weeks and, when you consider the dividing, feeding, dusting or spraying, pruning and disbudding they often need to be maintained in good condition, they are really no less work than annuals. Once planted and nursed with shade and water until they have established themselves, most annuals will repay you by producing faithfully until frost.

Besides, what flower lover could pass a summer without calendulas, zinnias, marigolds, mignonette, verbena, petunias, nasturtiums, cosmos or asters to play with? Or resist having the spires of larkspur, snapdragons and stock to frame graceful summer bouquets? Or look forward to autumn without a few home-grown strawflowers drying in various stages of openness?

I have not attempted to make a comprehensive list of what you can grow to give pleasure outdoors and in; to do that alone would take a longer book than this. These are only suggestions of what can be done. They should be rearranged, changed or disregarded to suit your own climate, home and tastes.

There are a few points you should keep in mind when you cut flowers from your garden if you want to enjoy them for the longest possible period of time. Cut flowers in as tight buds as you can, although this varies from species to species and you may have to experiment a little before you find the best moment to cut each of the different flowers you grow. Peonies can be cut when they are still hard-furled balls showing a few coloured petals at the top and will open to full size. Irises, too, can be cut when very tight and just showing colour.

Flowers which grow in spray formations, such as bulb lilies, miniature carnations and pompon chrysanthemums, open in sequence, the first two from the bottom of the stalk to the top, the last from top to bottom. If you cut them

when they are too tight, the green buds generally will not develop, so you will get more if you wait until the primary flowers are open and most of the buds show some colour.

Cut flower stems at a slanting angle, not straight across, with a sharp knife if possible. If you use scissors or clippers, make sure they are razor-sharp and do not mash the stem. Even with woody stems which you will slit or smash later to condition them to draw water, you need to make a sharp, smooth initial cut for the sake of the health of the tree or plant. A jagged, many-faceted surface is an invitation to pests.

Try to cut with an eye to a plant's future production of flowers. This involves two quite different techniques. With plants which are not prolific bloomers, you will want to spare all the buds you can for future use. It may involve a real sacrifice of developing buds to get a stem long enough for a spot in a special arrangement. On the other hand, with plants which are profuse in their growth and flowering habits, such as pansies, sweet peas and marigolds, you need not feel the least guilty. The more you lop away (within reason), the more you encourage a busy, shapely plant and healthy future production of buds. If you have time, snip off any dead flower heads as you go. Producing seeds wastes a plant's strength and ability to set future flowers; annuals think they have completed their life cycle and may give up the ghost, and

perennials and biennials will not bother to bear the second crop of which they may be capable.

Wilting caused by water loss is the greatest danger to cut flowers. To avoid this, cut when it is cool, moist and there is no wind, either before the sun is well up in the morning sky or after it has set in the evening and the day's heat has passed. Some experts recommend carrying pails, jars and cans of water with you in the garden so that you can plunge flowers in the instant they are cut. This may work well in compact, level gardens, but I have never found it very satisfactory in my rambling, hilly one. A pail of water is awkward and it sloshes. Until you have collected a fairly large bunch, the flowers are likely to tumble about and damage themselves. Besides, if you condition the flowers properly when you get them in the house, putting them into water in the garden should not really be necessary.

I prefer to use a long, shallow garden basket, not for its picturesque appearance but for its utility. With it I can move about the garden quickly and easily, putting the flowers in it in shallow layers. The heads of the flowers in an upper layer rest on the stems in a line beneath the heads of those in a lower layer, so there is a minimum of crushing or tangling of petals. If it is very hot, or dry and windy, a layer of damp newspaper in the bottom of the basket, and a few damp pages between each layer and over the top, helps prevent wilting.

Cut flowers should be gently placed in a basket in alternate layers, with damp newspaper at the bottom to prevent wilting.

Above : wild flowers and
grasses growing
along the edge of a
field. 'Weeds' like these
look very fresh and
delicate in a summer
arrangement.

Right : a mass arrange-
ment glowing with the
gold of late summer
gardens and fields.
Black-eyed Susans,
goldenrod, small sun-
flowers and lilies in a
cork bark container
which looks like a tree
stump.

Wild flowers and 'weeds'

The distinction between weeds and cultivated flowers is not always very clear. One old gardening joke claims that a weed is any plant growing where you do not want it, while a converse one has it that a garden flower is simply a weed which is expensive and difficult to grow. These are obvious exaggerations, but when you study the delicacy and elegance of such weeds or wild flowers as Queen Anne's lace (wild carrot), harebells and honeysuckle, you begin to see some truth in them.

If you delve into the history of flowers, your confusion will only grow. The original forms of all flowers obviously once grew wild until men saw them, loved them for the beauty of their appearance, their fragrance or their utility and moved them closer to their homes. In classical art and literature we find evidence that such flowers as roses, anemones, tulips, carnations, morning glory and narcissi had already established themselves in men's affections. Their fortunes waxed and waned in Europe during the Middle Ages. The tulip, native to Asia, reappears in Italian art as early as A.D. 1100, but Holland and northern Europe do not seem to have known it until the sixteenth century. The cabbage rose (*Rosa centifolia*), on the other hand, disappeared from Italy during the medieval period and was later re-introduced from Holland. Lilac, jasmine and hyacinths were brought to Europe from the East at the end of the Middle Ages.

One of the results of the voyages of exploration in the Renaissance was the migration of American 'weeds' and their cultivation in European gardens. From the sixteenth century through to the nineteenth, such flowers as marigolds, nasturtiums, sunflowers, zinnias, dahlias, agave (century plant) and nicotiana, among dozens of others, moved east across the Atlantic from Central and North America, while carefully transported garden flowers and weed seeds (such as those of cinquefoil and wild carrot), stowed away in sacks of grain, moved west.

The traffic still goes on. Such garden and florists' favourites as coreopsis, *Phlox drummondi*, gaillardia and liatris are wild flowers native to the American prairie. Some of these species have travelled to England and the Continent for breeding before returning to American gardens. A flower which is considered 'wild' or a 'weed' in one time and place may become a garden treasure in another.

We should not ignore a flower because we know it is a weed, but should study it carefully to discover its true quality. Wild flowers vary as widely in form, colour, texture, abundance of bloom, lasting potential and 'feeling' as cultivated ones do. Many of them are superb arranging flowers. I have already mentioned my admiration for Queen Anne's lace (*Daucus carota*). I inherited it from my grandmother, an expert gardener,

Purple loosestrife

Clover

Dog rose

Right: daisies and field grass arranged simply in a basket look at home almost anywhere.

who long ago shocked her college community by using it as a centrepiece for a formal dinner party. I prefer this flower to gypsophila (baby's breath) as a companion for aristocratic roses. Summer wild flowers, in particular, make a glowing bouquet which brings the countryside into your home, and they will last as well as sturdy garden annuals.

The spring woodland flowers are in general more delicate in appearance than midsummer field flowers and not as long-lasting, but, properly treated, their beauty can be treasured indoors for several days. Dutchman's breeches (*Dicentra cucullaria*), despite the amusing name given them because the florets look like tiny white pantaloons hung on the line to dry, have a pure elegance which rivals that of lily-of-the-valley and freesia. Their foliage is appropriately fine, almost fern-like. Unfortunately, Nature does not often spread them out in carpets as she does meadow chickweed (*Cerastium arvense*), wood violets (*Viola sylvestris*) and harebells (*Campanula rotundifolia*).

Which brings us to a vital point. This is a book on flower arranging, on the joys of bringing flowers into your home, but there are certain flowers you should leave right where they are. Some species of wild flowers are endangered, or are becoming so. To pluck up one of these should sting a flower lover's conscience as much as shooting a bald eagle would a bird lover's.

Information on endangered species is available, but the best guide is your own common sense. If you find great stands of yarrow, wild asters, loosestrife, daisies, clover or wild lupins, along the road or in a field, you know you can take home a good armful without endangering them. But if you find three or four dog-tooth violets pricking up from a woodland floor, you know the best thing to do would be to enjoy them for a moment and leave them where they are. If you are torn between pangs of conscience about the modest size of a patch of wild flowers and an irresistible urge to possess some of them, limit yourself to one or two sprays for a bud vase.

When we were children my brother and I made annual spring pilgrimages into the woods with our father to pick

Dutchman's breeches, violets, wild geraniums and columbine. We brought home bunches as large as we could carry to our mother. Years later when I was home at the right season, I went to look for our flowers. The violets still lined the ditch at the bottom of the mountain. The wild geranium and columbine still nodded in the open woods to the north, but on the rocky south-western slopes where there had once been a good number of spreading colonies of Dutchman's breeches, I could find only a few scattered plants. This may have been partially due to the onslaught of a

Queen Anne's lace

Harebell

Ox-eye daisy

Honeysuckle

creeping tangle of wild honeysuckle, but my conscience still pricks. What a waste, especially since my mother has always enjoyed looking at one or two perfect blossoms in a bud vase rather than coping with mass arrangements.

Pursuing the subject of ethics and common sense just a little further, keep in mind that almost all land belongs to someone, if not to an individual then to the State. If there is any place to ask permission to pick flowers, then ask, even if you feel a bit embarrassed.

If you are on public parkland it is wise to know the laws. Not the slightest harm will be done, however, if you gather to your heart's content along the side of a road that is doomed to be widened or in a lot where surveyors are marking out a shopping centre. Most people are fairly reasonable. They will not mind you picking a few flowers on their uncultivated land. The fact that you ask permission goes a long way towards showing them that you are not a vandal.

When you know you will be gathering wild flowers, go prepared. If you have a long drive home, a partially filled pail of water wedged on the floor of the back of the car, out of direct sunlight and wind, will help bring tall or bushy flowers home in something like their original state. Plastic bags with moisture in them are good for smaller varieties. Carry the same cutting equipment with you that you would use at home.

I have not mentioned trees and shrubs

Wood violet

up to this point, but they are as tempting as herbaceous wild flowers, and just as much to be protected. To rip branches off dogwood, holly, rhododendron, etc. and leave them open to the invasions of disease and pests is a poor way to repay them for the beauty they give.

One answer if you really love wild flowers is to grow them. Even city dwellers can grow quite a wide range of small flowers in a window box. The main thing is to grow what is natural to your climate and type of land. Given the environment for which Nature designed them, and left undisturbed by bulldozers and too many busy-fingered humans, most wild flowers are tough. There are varieties to grow everywhere, even where trees and grass will not take root.

Your conscience should guide you in obtaining plants for a wild garden just as in picking the flowers. Do not take a plant, and certainly not one of an endangered species, from where it is doing well unless you know what it needs and have a good home prepared for it. Do not take plants from public parklands and do ask the permission of private owners.

One advantage of growing your own wild flowers is that if you wish to use them for an exhibition in a flower show you can do so without fear of censure or disqualification by properly conservation-minded judges. Another (and, to me, more important) advantage is that you can enjoy them in your home without a qualm.

Tools of the Trade

Lilacs massed with pale to deep pink and purple tulips (Parrots, Darwins) in an old Chinese bronze and enamel container. Even though this vase holds a great deal of water, the level would have to be checked frequently to make sure the thirsty lilacs had not drunk it dry.

Conditioning

When you get your flowers into the house from garden, florist's shop, field or forest, the great temptation is to charge ahead and start trying to arrange them into the lovely picture that has been growing in your mind as you chose them. If you are racing a deadline, such as the arrival of guests, this temptation may become a necessity. In this case, try to do the minimum: recut the bottoms of the stems with a sharp knife or scissors and put the flowers in as deep water as you can manage with the proportions of your arrangement.

If you are not in a hurry, prepare the flowers properly and let them draw water. They will repay you for your efforts by lasting much longer. The proof of this is the amount of time and effort professional florists spend on conditioning their stock. Flowers are a serious matter with them. They do not have time for non-essential fussing, but they have to do everything they can to make their product last in their shops and in their customers' homes. If it does, they are successful merchants: if it does not, they are bankrupt.

Flowers which have been conditioned and have drawn sufficient water at the florist's, and which have been brought straight home without being exposed to heat or given a chance to dry out, will not need much attention. Cut the stems as you arrange them, or put them in water until you are ready to do so. Cut flowers which are delivered from a florist are a different matter, however, particularly in holiday seasons. They

may have spent considerable time out of water, waiting for the driver to load them and then bouncing around in the van on a long delivery run. These you had better inspect to see what reconditioning may be necessary.

The basic idea behind conditioning flowers is very simple. When a flower is cut it is deprived of its normal supply of water and you have to make sure that it quickly resumes drawing enough water without impediment to prevent wilting. There are various processes to ensure this, some of them specialized because of the composition of certain types of plants. Then you follow this up by placing the flower in a situation where the least possible evaporation will occur from surfaces exposed to the air.

Almost all flowers benefit from the removal of foliage that will be below the waterline. Leaves rot quickly under water, especially those of flowers such as marigolds, daisies and chrysanthemums. This not only causes an evil-smelling, ugly mess, the bacteria in it will attack and weaken the stems.

You should also remove any excess foliage above the waterline. The flowers at the tips of the stem are at the 'end of the line' for receiving water and if there are too many leaves below taking their share first, the flowers will suffer. This is particularly true of shrubs such as lilac. If the foliage is decorative and you wish to use it in your arrangement, take it off the stem and put it in water separately. Cut a few flowerless sprays for height.

I **am not** suggesting denuding all stems. **That** would be unattractive and unnecessary. However, in exceptional cases (for example, when you want to take an arrangement of chrysanthemums or daisies, whose leaves wither far faster than the blossoms, to a hospital where it will get scant attention) it may be best to remove all major foliage and soften the arrangement with something long-lasting, such as leather fern.

Cut the bottom of stems with a sharp knife on a slanting diagonal line. A diagonal cut exposes more of the surface of the stem to water than if you cut straight across. The point also keeps the stem from resting flat on the bottom of the container and blocking free access to water. This treatment should be given to most flowers from the very tenderest-stemmed, such as violets, lily-of-the-valley, and forget-me-nots, through the average zinnias, snapdragons, gladioli etc., to some quite hard stems like peonies and roses. I will deal with the exceptions, the tough fibrous stems of flowers like chrysanthemums, later.

Flowers with jointed stems, such as carnations, baby's breath, sweet william and phlox, should be given their slanting cuts just above a joint.

When heavy knobs remain after foliage or side shoots have been stripped away from flowers such as peonies, the knobs should be sliced off flush with the surface of the stem. The same can be done with thorns on roses. This increases the ability of the stems to draw

Tulips supported by a tube of newspaper to straighten the stems.

water, but only if done below the waterline. Above it it has the opposite effect.

Some bulbs, such as daffodils, narcissi and hyacinths, have a slimy sap which oozes out when they are cut. It is a good idea to wipe this off the ends before putting them in water, so that the water passages will be kept clean.

The stems of other flowers, such as poppies, euphorbia (poinsettia is the best known of this genus, although not the best for arranging) and heliotrope, have a sticky white sap. If it is allowed to drain out when they are cut, the flowers will wilt. To prevent the loss of sap, seal the stem ends by singeing them in an open flame or scalding them in boiling water.

Flowers with tough, fibrous stems, such as chrysanthemums of all types, asters, stock and heather, should have the skin scraped below the waterline and their stem ends roughly broken off, rather than sharply sliced. Professional florists scrape by holding the stem in their off hand, a knife handle curled in the fingers of their working hand with the blade pressed against the stem at an upward angle and their thumb bracing the stem right behind the blade. They draw their knife hand along the stem, peeling away skin and foliage and breaking off the stem bottom at the end of the movement. They turn the stem, repeating the scraping motion two or three times, and the flower is 'cleaned'

in a matter of a few seconds. With a little practice, you will find this a very quick and easy method, but if it scares you or if you do not want a green-black-stained 'florist's thumb', just pretend the stem is a very fragile carrot and scrape it carefully any way you find easy.

Although daisies may not seem very tough-stemmed, they benefit enormously from being scraped. Their stem ends, however, should be cut rather than broken.

Flowering wood branches, especially lilac, should be given even rougher treatment. They should have their bottoms broken, deeply slit, or, better still, smashed with a hammer so that the large amounts of water which they require can get into the tough stems.

The procedures described above may seem complicated, but once you get the hang of them they will take less time to do than to read about. Besides, you will rarely have to use all the techniques to prepare one group of flowers.

The moment you have sliced, scraped, smashed or singed a flower stem, plunge it immediately into deep, clean water. If the end of the stem or the scraped area dries out, the flower cannot draw water easily and your work will have been in vain. I was once told by a botany instructor at college that the best procedure of all would be to cut stems under water. This is generally too messy a method to be practical (rose stems do not look nice lying at the bottom of a crystal vase and imagine trying to smash lilac stems under water!), and I have not found that flowers suffer as long as they are put into water promptly after being handled.

There has been a good deal of discussion at one time or another about the proper water temperature in which to condition flowers, and about chemical additives which may increase their lifespan. I do not think that in practice water temperature makes a great difference to flowers, although extremes, hot or icy water, do no good. Flowers seem to do well in any reasonable water temperature, from tepid to cool. As for additives, some of the theories, such as 'Give your roses two aspirin', do actual mischief. The commercially prepared formulas certainly do no harm and may actually benefit flowers but, as far as I have been able to observe, not very dramatically.

More important than water temperature or additives is to place flowers in

sufficient water in proper containers. In most cases, 'sufficient' water means deep water, roughly one half to three quarters of the stem length. The exceptions to this are most of the bulb flowers. They should be put in shallower water since their petals seem to become 'papery' faster in deep water. Containers should be of the right size and, above all, clean. Do not jam short-stemmed flowers in with tall ones. They are likely to be crushed, particularly when you move them or try to get them out, and if you are not careful the big flowers may drink so much that the level drops below the point where the little ones can reach it. Make sure there is no residue from soap or other household cleaning agents and no debris from past flowers left in the containers. Copper containers release a chemical in water which has a bad effect on roses, but seems to strengthen tulip stems.

Foliage you are going to use in arrangements should be conditioned in the same way as flowers. Some leaves, such as ivy, *Vinca minor* and ferns, benefit

Scraping the stem of a chrysanthemum. Hold the stem in your 'off' hand and draw the knife firmly towards you.

from being completely submerged for a while.

If you want flowers or foliage to take on particular curves or bends for an arrangement you have in mind, this is the time to persuade them to do it. They will be less amenable once they have drawn water. Flowering branches, such as pussy willow, podocarpus and broom, can be gently shaped by hand to the line you desire and fastened in place with wire. When the wire is removed after they have been in water overnight, the curve will hold. If stock, snapdragon, tulips, anemones, etc., are placed in water with their stems on a fairly horizontal plane and their heads supported by the rim of the container, the tips will turn up naturally toward the light, making the stalks curve.

If you want to achieve straight stems with flowers which are not always obliging that way (tulips, for example), wrap the flowers, heads and all, in a tube of newspaper and secure it with rubber bands before putting in deep water.

This technique, coupled with a fresh cut on the stem, is also good first aid for flowers which are wilting. When roses' heads bow over before their time they often do not seem to be able to pull water past the bend, but if they are given a long drink with their heads supported by the paper tube, they frequently reappear the next morning with a new lease of life.

Once your flowers are in water, they should be put in a cool place away from direct sunlight and draughts and left undisturbed for several hours or, if possible, overnight.

Keeping flowers away from heat and draughts is important, not only when you are conditioning them, but also after you have completed your arrangement. The evaporation of moisture from petals and leaves caused by heat and draughts can negate the work you have done to make sure your flowers drank enough water to withstand wilting.

Arranging is a much more satisfactory experience with properly conditioned flowers than with unconditioned ones. For one thing, you have more latitude. You can safely make Oriental line arrangements in shallow containers. Also, you rarely have to worry about changing the water or pulling out stems to recut them (an invitation to disaster). Check every day or two to make sure the water is up to the proper level, snip out any dead blossoms with scissors and enjoy your handiwork.

Containers

Having properly treated the flowers and left them to draw water, what should you put them in? This need not be either a dull or a difficult problem as long as you remember that not everything labelled 'vase' was designed to hold flowers gracefully. And the opposite is also true. Many things originally designed for other uses make ideal vases.

Collecting flower containers can become a fascinating hobby. Once you have caught the bug, it is hard to pass the window of a secondhand or antique shop without stopping to see 'what there is'. You can spend as much time, money and storage space on it as you can afford. A shelf of vases can grow into a cupboard or closet.

However, you do not *need* a large collection of containers. People who do have large collections often find themselves coming back time and again to certain favourites, leaving the rest on the shelf to be used only occasionally.

These peony stems have been cut diagonally with a sharp knife so that only the tip rests on the bottom of the container and they can take up more water. All the foliage below the water-line has been removed and only a few leaves higher up have been left for decoration.

23

If you are starting to collect containers, no set of rules will guarantee that the first ones you buy will end up being your favourites, the ones in which flowers always seem to look 'right' in certain spots in your home. Having said that, there are still a few basic points which may increase the odds of your making a good choice.

Bear in mind the general style of your home. This should come naturally, if your home reflects, as it should, your personal interests and taste. Hunt for containers in the same sort of shops as those that sell the furnishings with which you like to surround yourself. But never turn a blind eye when you are in alien territory. You may love eighteenth-century antiques and yet find just the vase you have needed, with simple classical lines, in a shop selling twentieth-century crystal. Or, to reverse the case, your home may be strictly modern yet gracefully accept the counterpoint of an old pewter bowl or a beaten copper pitcher.

When considering the size and shape of containers, think about where you will be using them. Certain spots in your home 'ask' for flowers, and these spots themselves dictate the proportions of the vases you can use in them.

For centrepieces, low bowls are most generally useful, round for round or square dining tables (I find square containers very awkward for centrepieces), oval for long tables. An alternative idea is a series of small bowls or short vases which can be placed in an irregular line along the length of the table. Or you might try to find some of the wonderful tall Edwardian bud vases. They rise in slender columns which do not interfere seriously with the line of vision and you can put sprays of lilac or euphorbia in them to spread like a canopy over the heads of your guests.

For hall tables, sideboards, etc., roughly measure the area you want an arrangement to cover. The rule of thumb is that the container should be one-third to two-fifths of the height of the total arrangement. You may want two different types of vase for spots like these. One choice is a footed or pedestalled vase for shorter flowers or those which do not require very deep water. For 'thirsty' and heavier flowers you should also have a vase that uses its full height for holding water. A base, such as a slab of polished wood, sometimes helps give visual weight to this type of heavy container.

When an arrangement is going to be placed near or above eye level, as on a mantelpiece or a shelf, the rule about the proportion of container height to arrangement does not apply. Medieval sculptors working on the facades of cathedrals discovered that the legs of statues had to be foreshortened to make the figure appear normal from ground level. The same principles hold good in flower arranging: what is in proportion on a low table does not look in proportion if you are looking up at it. Shallow containers, sometimes with a low foot, seem to me to be the best answer for mantelpieces and shelves. Matching urns or vases on either side of a mantel are old favourites and can look wonderful in period homes. The trick is to keep the containers from dominating the flowers and the arrangements from visually overloading the mantelpiece, and for this the proportioning has to be carefully worked out.

Left: double yellow tulips in a highly ornamental Chinese caddy.
Right: the pink and white container has been repeated with an arrangement of lilies and cosmos.

24

You may have a spot where very tall branches of spring blossom, leaves or autumn foliage would look well rising from floor level. (This can be a good answer to the dark corners where some decorators insist on putting large plants that will not thrive.) For this you need a tall vase which holds plenty of water and which, above all, is heavy and of a good stable design.

You will probably want a few bowls and vases for coffee and bedside tables and desks, or wherever you may feel like having a bright splash of colour. If you love tiny things, as I do, you can have great fun collecting containers for miniature arrangements. I have a very personal objection to surrounding them with doll's furnishing accessories. Their smallness, which is what is special about them, seems to me better accentuated when they are in normal-sized surroundings.

The colour and texture of the containers you choose should, like the shape and size, add to the interest of your arrangements, but never dominate them. You are safest choosing the neutral shades which go best with your own colour scheme. Black, white, off-whites, browns, soft greens or greys will be the most generally useful because they will not compete with the colours of the flowers you choose. It is also safer to avoid distinctive decoration on a vase.

Of course, the safest way is not always the most interesting way to achieve success. A mass of daisies looks marvellous in a brightly coloured modern container and many of the loveliest old china vases and bowls are patterned. One of the prettiest centrepieces I can remember making was done in an oval vegetable dish with a design of flowers in shades of soft reds and off-whites. When it was first brought in by one of my favourite customers I did not know what I was going to do with it, but I assured

her that I would think of something. The answer was short sprays cut from a branch of dogwood, combined with small red pencil tulips, anemones in softer shades of red and white narcissi. The flowers repeated the colours and shapes of those in the vegetable dish pattern, but on a larger scale so that they gave an effect of having grown out of the pattern almost naturally. If the flowers in the pattern had been large, I would have had a more difficult problem in keeping the container from dominating the arrangement.

Some flowers (and some backgrounds) seem better suited to containers of certain types of material than others. Choosing a container for a flower is like choosing a dress for a woman. You have to take personality as well as looks into account. Annuals such as marigolds, calendulas and zinnias look more comfortable in homely containers of pottery, wood or copper. More formal flowers such as roses, lilies or delphinium look better in vases or bowls of crystal, silver or porcelain.

Wild flowers are often labelled as homely types to be put in unpretentious containers, but I think that this is much too general a classification to be true. Wild roses are no more intimidated by crystal than garden ones, and Dutchman's breeches and wild columbine seem to me too delicately wrought to be at home in a mug.

A great many vases are made of crystal and clear glass. Transparent vases are best reserved for flowers which arrange easily and whose stems are attractive and do not decay quickly under water. Otherwise you run into the problem of masking your arranging materials and perhaps the stems also. This can be done, but it is easier to avoid the problem by having only a few clear vases of very good design to use for simple arrangements of such flowers as roses and spring bulbs. Wide-mouthed vases need arranging aids to stop the flowers tumbling about, so I usually try to find

clear vases with small openings or ones which narrow not too far below the lip.

Baskets are about the most versatile of all containers. I have always loved them and am glad that they have become popular again. They seem to be equally at ease in the kitchen or the drawing room, filled with marigolds or carnations. You can buy them at a florist's shop already fitted with tin or plastic liners. The problem with tin liners is that after a certain amount of exposure to water they rust through in spots and their sharp edges sometimes cut tender-stemmed flowers. You can retard rusting by spraying with plastic or paint, but if a basket becomes a real favourite a more permanent solution is to find the right size of plastic bowl or food storage container. Antique stores and auctions sometimes have old baskets with wonderful colour and feeling. It is usually wiser to choose an open shape. Lidded ones, such as fishing creels and sewing baskets, present difficulties when arranging and are generally less useful. Open-work baskets are very attractive if you line them with sheet moss before inserting the waterproof container. You can get the moss in rolls at a florist's.

If you come across something which would make an ideal vase for your home but which does not hold water or would be damaged by it, do not give up. Cracks and small holes in china and glass can be repaired by a number of different methods, sometimes by simply applying a strip of plastic florist's clay. For wood and other containers you can find liners just as you would for baskets. Almost anything can be made to hold water, but the main points to consider are whether the shape, colour, texture, size and feeling of the container will complement flowers in the setting of your home.

Equipment

Apart from flowers and containers, there is some basic equipment which helps to make arranging easy and pleasant. A trip to a hardware store and to a good florist's should provide you with most of it.

A good knife is essential. Choose one that balances comfortably in your hand. I have an ordinary jack-knife, the blade kept razor sharp. One snap and there is no danger from the blade when it is not is use. Since I have a small son with quick and curious fingers, this seems an important asset to me. Some people prefer a larger, fixed-bladed knife with a sheath. It is simply a matter of what you can work with most comfortably and efficiently. The main point is that the blade, whatever its size and shape, should be kept really sharp. A dull one may make sloppy cuts on stems and will certainly make your work slower and harder. You might find it handy to keep a small sharpener with your equipment.

Some people prefer to work entirely with scissors. A knife is really more practical for most of the cleaning and scraping you have to do, and in cutting stems you avoid the danger of crushing rather than opening the vessels that carry water. Even if you work mainly with a knife, however, you will need a good sharp pair of scissors for occasional jobs such as trimming brown edges from a leaf or cutting ribbon for Christmas or other decorations.

You will find a good pair of garden shears handy for cutting the heavy wood stems of flowering branches, autumn foliage, rhododendrons, etc.

The mechanical aids which man's ingenuity has contrived for holding flowers in place in a vase are so numerous that I will not even attempt to list them.

They range from the forked stick (*kubari*) of classical Japanese arrangements to modern blocks of plastic foam. I will describe a few which I think you may find the most useful and easy to obtain.

Pinholders are a mass of tiny spikes set in a lead base, usually painted green. You may want a collection of these in different sizes and shapes to fit your containers. Do not bother buying the lightweight ones set in plastic bases. They will tip about and give you more aggravation than help. For your larger containers, in which you will be using taller, heavier flowers, try to get the pinholders which are set in cages. These give you two points of support for stems: at the base where they are sunk on the pins, and 2–3 inches further up. You may want to anchor pinholders permanently in the containers you use most often. I do not do this, unless it is necessary to increase stability, because it makes them difficult to clean, and clean containers are a vital element in preserving the life of your flowers.

If you do want to anchor pinholders, use florist's plastic stickum. This is a modern replacement for the old florist's clay. It comes in a roll with the flattened strip of sticky plastic ready to be pulled off in pieces from between layers of heavy wax paper. Whether or not you are anchoring pinholders, this is very useful stuff to have. It will fasten objects together instantly and quite firmly.

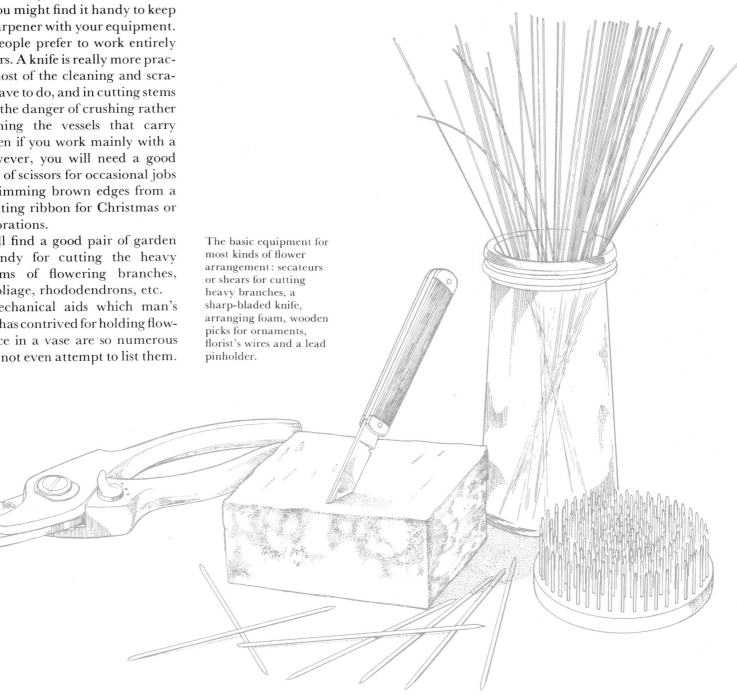

The basic equipment for most kinds of flower arrangement: secateurs or shears for cutting heavy branches, a sharp-bladed knife, arranging foam, wooden picks for ornaments, florist's wires and a lead pinholder.

Make sure that any surface to which you want it to adhere is perfectly clean and dry.

Plastic arranging foam is a valuable contribution of modern science to the art of flower arrangement. It has its limitations, but generally it is the quickest and easiest medium for arranging and, when properly used, it does not seem to shorten the lifespan of most cut flowers. You can buy it from your florist in bricks.

There are a number of different brands of foam. Unlike many things sold today, there is a real difference between the brands, as I proved to my own satisfaction by experimentation while working as a florist. The most common brand has a heavy consistency which is fine for the tougher flowers after they have been properly conditioned and have drawn water. For more tender flowers, a foam with a lighter consistency is better; the softer stems go in easily and the flowers seem to hold up well. Choose the foams which are dark moss-green in colour, so that you will not have to deal with the camouflage problem which a lighter, bluish one presents. Avoid any brand that makes you feel

that you are trying to sink a stem into a wad of soggy cottonwool.

Foam is not a good medium for the tenderest flowers, such as forget-me-nots, violets and pansies. If you want to use a clump of them in an arrangement you are making in foam, bunch them together with string or tape and insert them in a pocket dug out of the foam, so that their stems are surrounded by water.

When you buy the foam it is dry. The most practical way to handle it is to cut off a piece the size you need and store the remainder of the block. Make sure that the foam you are using is thoroughly soaked, and that there are no stray air bubbles still rising from it. The lighter consistency foams absorb water much more quickly than the heavier ones.

You may have to 'tailor' the foam to fit your container. You can make graceful arrangements more easily if the foam rises slightly above the rim of the container, because you can then angle flowers and leaves down over the edge without difficulty. If you are using a deep bowl, you may need a pad of foam underneath to bring the main block to the right height. Sometimes you may

Above: lily-of-the-valley in a pedestalled clear glass bowl. A grid of tape (see page 31) was used to arrange these rather short, early lilies-of-the-valley. If you were seated at the table you would see the delicate stems, but not the mechanics which hold them in place.

Right: a workbench laid out with equipment for a spring arrangement. The head of a globe artichoke is wired for a dry arrangement and several lemons have been pierced with florist's wire to release their refreshing smell which mingles deliciously with the scent of spring flowers. Dried and fresh fruit can add an unusual touch to a table centrepiece but needs careful wiring.

also need wedge-shaped pieces to fill out the width. Rarely, however, does a container have to be solidly crammed with foam to provide a stable and convenient base for arranging. This would be messy when you tried to add water and, in the case of large vases, expensive. You can often wedge a block of foam securely in the top of tall vases. If you cannot do it, the vase is obviously not a good one in which to use foam.

It is just as important when you are using foam as when you are not to check the water level daily and to keep containers filled to the brim. It is easy to forget this, but that way lies disaster. Foam is not a magic substance; it can only do its work when you provide it with water.

I have read a great many warnings against re-using foam, but I have done it often myself with no bad results. I have never seen reasons given for the warning, but I imagine the theory is that holes from previous use might create air pockets. If you surround a used block with water, however, the holes will fill right to the water level. The point, then, is to keep the water level well up. After a number of usings, depending on the size of the block and the type of stems that have been inserted in it, the foam will be so pierced that it

is in danger of breaking apart. Obviously it should then be discarded. Until it reaches this point, however, I see no reason not to save money by re-using foam.

When you have your foam in place, secure it with arranging tape. This is another many-purposed item which you can buy at a florist's. It is green cloth-backed adhesive tape which comes in $\frac{1}{2}$-inch width rolls. You rarely need the full width to do a secure job, so you can save tape and leave yourself more arranging surface if you slit the end of the tape in the middle and tear one side along in a $\frac{1}{4}$-inch width.

Make sure the outside of the rim of your container is dry before you press the tape onto it. If the surface is damp, the tape will slip. When this happens, heat the spot where you want to secure the tape and run a match over the back of the tape. This should give you a firm seal. Two pieces of tape stretched tightly across the top of your container at right angles to each other will secure the foam so that you need not worry about it slipping while you work.

Florist's tape can occasionally help to solve awkward arranging problems. For instance, if you want to make a loose, airy arrangement of lily-of-the-valley, instead of bunching it, the stems are so fine that a pinholder is not much

help and foam is out. Take $\frac{1}{4}$-inch strips of tape and make a grid across the top of your container, securing the ends with another piece around the circumference. It takes a little time, but it does solve the problem.

Although many people work quite well with chicken wire, I consider it a frustrating nuisance, at least in the way it has traditionally been used in flower arranging. Trying to work with a crushed tangle of it reduces me to swearing, because where I want a stem to go there is invariably a wire blocking it at some point, and then when I have coaxed the stem past the obstruction the flower is rarely placed at the angle I had intended. There are moments, however, when chicken wire is helpful. If you are working with heavy branches or very large-stemmed flowers, such as gladioli, pinholders are inadequate and an un-reinforced block of foam is likely to crack. Fit a piece of chicken wire over the foam and secure it around the edge of the container with wire or tape, and you should have a strong enough base.

An inexpensive but essential item which you can obtain at a florist's is green wire in various weights. I have heard people say that wiring flowers seems 'cruel'. If they are talking about some of the more hideous examples of corsages, I agree that there is at least a visual impression of torture. There are situations, though, where wire can save a flower which you might otherwise discard. When the head of a cornflower, say, has been bent over but not broken, a wire inserted a short way into the base of the head and run down through the

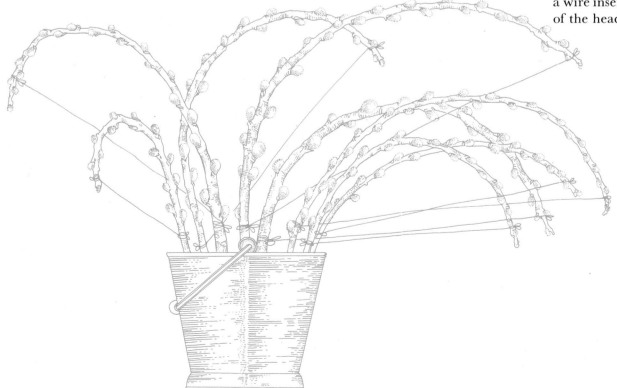

Left: branches of pussy willow can be made to curve if they are gently bent into shape, wired in position and left overnight in deep water.

Florist's tape can be used in a grid as a support for arranging delicate flowers, especially tender-stemmed spring flowers. Secure the ends of tape with a separate strip of tape round the outside rim of the container.

The finished arrangement of lily-of-the-valley is shown in the photograph on page 28.

stem will support the head so that it not only looks nice but can also get water which was previously blocked by the bend in the stem.

Wires are handy in so many ways, particularly in making Christmas decorations, that I cannot even begin to list their uses. You can get them in a range of different gauges, and you will probably find it useful to have three weights (light, medium and heavy) on hand for different jobs. You might also want to get a spool of green wire. While we are on the subject, you might consider buying a wire cutter before you aggravate yourself (or someone else) by ruining a pair of scissors hacking away at wire.

Florist's corsage tape and green wooden picks have their uses all year round and are invaluable at Christmas. Instead of trying to wire cones and ornaments into position in arrangements, you can tape the wire holding them onto wooden picks and jab them quickly and

securely in place. Corsage tape, which is rather like waxy green crêpe paper, comes in ½-inch wide rolls. You use it by stretching it firmly down and around two things you want to fasten together (a wire and a stem, a wood pick and an ornament handle), and seal it by pressing it onto itself.

A sheet or two of plastic (the bags cleaners put over dresses will do) may come in handy. The few seconds it takes to put a sheet over your work surface can save minutes later when you are cleaning up.

Once you have acquired the equipment you need, it is a good idea to keep it together in one place. The more thought you give to organizing in a way that works efficiently for you, the less time will be wasted later looking for things. I like to keep my basic tools in a compartmented basket so that I can pick the whole thing up and move it to where I want to work on an arrangement. To each his or her own system.

The Principles of Flower Arranging

This unusual elegant arrangement has an almost sculptural quality. The large flowers – gerbera, border carnations, and a single pansy – are placed in the centre, surrounded by columbine, candytuft, hosta, *Viburnum tinus* leaves and trailing stems of nicotiana.

Flower arranging should be a pleasure. The information given in the preceding chapters and the guidelines set down in this are aimed at helping you to achieve this end. Learning and practising good techniques should help you to avoid problems and create successful arrangements, but remember, there is no set of rules which define beauty and no single method for creating it. If a rule hinders rather than helps you, break it. (Sit back afterwards and try to figure out why it was necessary to break it. You often find that some other law of proportion, balance or harmony has come into play.) When, after practice, you decide that a suggested technique is a chore which does not yield sufficient dividends, discard it and experiment to find what will work for you.

What is a successful arrangement? It is one which is pleasing – above all, to you, the creator. Arrangements of any type need certain qualities to please the eye: shape, proportion, balance, depth (three-dimensionality), variety (interest in the combination of colours, shapes and textures of the flowers and foliage used) and a general harmony of all the parts. These are abstract terms which can be used to describe a successful finished arrangement. The problem is to translate them into reality in terms of tulips and lilac, marigolds and daisies.

Let us deal with shape first, because it leads quite naturally to a brief survey of the two major heritages of modern flower arrangement. The seeds of the present and future lie in the past, no matter how violently some innovators

may try to break away and declare their independence, so it is interesting and useful to know a little history.

Flower arrangements can be divided into two categories, line and mass. Within each category there are a variety of shapes, and both in the past and more frequently in modern times there has been a combining of the two categories into a third: line-mass.

Line arrangements are the traditional form of the Orient. At their best they are characterized by a clearly defined line seeking to represent the graceful irregularity of Nature through simplicity and great economy in the use of plant material. From early times flowers were placed in vases on the altars of China. They were important and developed deep symbolic meaning, but they were not used in profusion. In their philosophy and religion the Chinese sought to appreciate that which was tranquil and harmonious in Nature. They had great reverence for life in any form and tried to use it sparingly. Confucius taught that viewing too much beauty at one time was distracting and that true enjoyment lay in absorbing and savouring the beauty of one perfect thing. The Chinese applied this appreciation of simplicity quite naturally to the use of flowers in their temples and homes. A few sprays of seasonal flowers (plum blossom in winter, peonies in spring, lotus in summer or chrysanthemums in autumn), carefully placed in a beautiful container, were soul-satisfying to contemplate.

In the sixth century A.D., Chinese

missionary priests introduced Buddhism to Japan and with it the tradition of floral offerings. Japanese priests continued to develop and stylize the art of flower arranging. The famous Ikenobo School, which still flourishes today, was founded in the seventh century. The use of flowers spread from the temple to altars in the home. For a while arrangements grew larger and more complex, but by the fifteenth century the love of simplicity and stylization reasserted itself and the formal, classic Japanese arrangement of only three main lines springing from one focal point was established. This type of arrangement, called *Shoka* or *Ikenobo*, is the one which is the most widely known and influential in the West. It takes the shape of an asymmetrical triangle, the form of which is outlined by the tips of the three main branches. The three lines are known as Heaven, Earth and Man (*ten-chi-jin*).

The tall primary line, now called *Shin*, should be at least one and a half times the height of a tall container or the width of a flat one. It can be a good deal longer, depending on the visual weight of the spray. The tip of the primary branch should be directly over the point at which the base emerges from the container. Obviously a straight line between these two points is not the most graceful one, so the Orientals frequently choose a naturally curved branch, or with skill and patience bend one until it can make a charming visual journey from the high point to the base.

The secondary line, called *Soe*, should be two-thirds the length of the primary,

An arrangement of *Galax aphylla, Sansaveria trifasciata*, flower seed heads and magnolia leaves, illustrating the classic proportions of a *Shoka* arrangement.

Shin, line. The third and lowest, or Earth, line, called *Tai*, should be two-thirds the length of the *Soe* line. In less formal *Shoka* arrangements the *Tai* line may be replaced by a single flower or a small group of flowers. All three lines should appear to spring from one point. The tips of branches should curve up, not down or away from the observer.

Co-existing with the classic *Shoka* form, there have always been less formal types of arrangement. The ancient *Nageire* style, while it sought a subtle, natural appearance of flowers casually placed in a container, was still based on the shape of the asymmetrical triangle. So too is the more modern *Moribana* style, developed in this century. There are two types of *Moribana* arrangement, one based mainly on flowers, the other

creating miniature landscapes with branches, mosses and appropriate plant material. Both use low, flat containers and, if it is proper to the season being evoked, leave a large portion of the water open to act as a reflecting pool. Natural as these arrangements appear, they generally maintain the three basic elements and the shape of the asymmetrical triangle.

In this brief description, I have not even scratched the surface of the complexities of Oriental flower arranging. There are many other schools, and in the ones I have mentioned there are divisions and sub-divisions of styles. If you become interested in doing line arrangements, you will want to learn more. Anyone who wants to become a true master of Oriental flower arranging

has a lifetime's study before him. In the East, flower arrangement is an art and is bound inextricably to the other arts, to philosophy and to a whole attitude towards life which is different from ours.

In the West, a totally different type of arrangement evolved, the mass arrangement. I dislike the term 'mass', it sounds so lumpy, but it is the one commonly used to describe old-fashioned garden bouquets. A mass arrangement need not be massive. It can, and I think it should, be light and airy. It may be made of one type of flower, or of two or three, or of an infinite variety.

The most traditional shapes for mass arrangements are oval, circular and fan. In upright arrangements, such as one- or three-quarter-faced ones against a wall, or all-round ones on a piano, the oval or circle is vertical. In arrangements viewed from above, as on a dining or coffee table, it is horizontal.

Our knowledge of how flowers were used to ornament European homes in earlier days comes mainly from a study of the visual arts. Plants, their habits of growth and their uses as food and medicine, have been studied seriously from the time of the Greeks and Romans, but floral decoration has only achieved the status of an art in relatively modern times. This does not mean that Westerners did not love flowers or were unmoved by their beauty. I imagine that almost as soon as man learned to make vessels which would hold water, he began to put flowers in them to cheer whatever he used for a home. Flowers appeared as a motif early in European art. The Egyptians made much use of the lotus, the Greeks of the acanthus leaf. From the time of the Romans there are depictions of flowers massed together in profusion.

Flowers, however, never became closely linked with philosophy and religion in Europe as they did in the Orient. Perhaps this is because the Western mind seems to think less easily in terms of symbols than does the Eastern. The major exception to this sweeping generalization was the medieval period, when symbolism rose to its height in European thought, and flowers were included in the trend. Perhaps it is at this point that Occidental flower usage came closest to Oriental. In medieval paintings, particularly in Annunciations, one frequently sees a few sprays of flowers placed in a container and used symbolically (white flowers, such as lilies, snowdrops, lily-of-the-valley and iris stood for the purity of the Virgin: roses and clove pinks represented love, violets humility, three-leafed clover and tri-coloured pansies the Trinity, columbines the Holy Ghost). But no clear sense of line is developed, and, though the beauty of the flowers is painstakingly portrayed, their placement is always casual. One also often sees small mixed bouquets of garden flowers in medieval paintings.

When the great energy of the Renaissance burst across Europe, it swept away any tendency there may have been towards restraint in the use of flowers. Over the course of several centuries, the voyages of discovery brought back unknown plants from all corners of the world. Europeans promptly began to raise them and cut the flowers to combine with old garden favourites in massed arrangements. They may not have developed as fine a sense of the linear

beauty of flowers and foliage as Oriental arrangers, but they revelled in their colours and contrasts.

From the seventeenth to the nineteenth century, Europe and America remained loyal to the mass arrangement despite the influx of plants, art, ideas and even flower containers from the Orient. There are differences between the various periods, but they are mainly ones of scale, favoured flowers, colour combinations and containers. If you have a home built and furnished in the style of a particular period, you might have fun investigating what flowers could most authentically be grown in the garden and used in arrangements inside.

When we were given permission to use the American Wing of the Metropolitan Museum of Art for backgrounds to some of the photographs in this book, it was on the condition that the plant materials be as authentic to the period of the rooms as possible, and I became quite fascinated with the project. For the Samuel Powell Room (c. 1765), I discovered to my dismay that although we were photographing in the autumn I could not use any chrysanthemums because, except for feverfew, they were not grown in the West until the nineteenth century. But I could use ranunculas, stock, lilac and anemones, and miniature carnations made a pretty good substitute for clove gilly flowers. The more I researched, the more interested I became. A garden club or a group of individuals could make a project out of providing and arranging authentic plant material for a local museum or landmark.

There are some examples of line arrangements in Western art before 1900, for example, the Hogarth or lazy-S curve, but they show no Oriental influence, and in any case they never rivalled the popularity of the massed garden bouquet. It is only in the twentieth century that the asymmetrical triangle of the Japanese and their rules for proportion have had an impact on flower arranging in America and Europe. The impact was not lessened by

Left: a *Moribana* arrangement of chrysanthemums, using part of the water as a reflecting pool.

Overleaf, left: wild and garden flowers are skilfully combined in this delicate mass arrangement. The bunches of grapes and wild blackberries add a particularly Renaissance note.

Overleaf, right: a modern line arrangement of Birds of Paradise, gerbera and creamy spider chrysanthemums with broom and leaves.

The long low shape of this arrangement of dried flowers is in harmony with the proportions of the mantlepiece.

Overleaf, left: The exuberant explosion of flowers and rich mixing of varieties places Renoir's *Spring Bouquet* in the grand tradition of paintings of European mass arrangements. Although the placing of the flowers seems completely casual, there is a basic shape, an assymetrical triangle. *Overleaf, right:* a fragrant spring arrangement of lavender, wisteria, golden iris, freesia, viburnum and Spanish scilla.

being delayed. For several decades the line arrangement almost eclipsed the bouquet, though not in all hearts and homes, I think.

The adoption of new forms by a large group of people always has mixed results at first. At best, the advent of the line arrangement has given some people a fresh insight into the beauty of Nature, an appreciation of the linear rhythm of plants and a disciplined restraint which suits them. At worst, it has caused others to adhere to a set of rules and regulations without the least understanding of the sort of beauty they were designed to help create. The latter group, struggling laboriously to make flowers conform to the rules, have committed the stiff, tortured crimes against flower arranging that you see exhibited in some florists' shops and at some flower shows.

When one style sweeps another from vogue, the older one is likely to be rated below its true value for a while. The traditional bouquet of the West has been treated as a stepchild by some writers on flower arranging. They tend to gloss over it and to use the word 'art' sparingly in connection with it. Part of the problem is that there is not such a clearly defined code governing mass arrangement as there is for line arrangement, which makes it difficult to explain how to create successful arrangements and just as difficult to support one's judgement of which are good and which are not. It reminds me of Voltaire's quandary about Shakespeare's plays.

His instinct told him they were the works of a genius, but judging them by the classic Greek rules for unity in drama, in which he believed devoutly, he had great trouble in believing that they were art. Fortunately things readjust themselves in the long run. Few people nowadays question Shakespeare's worth, and there are hopeful signs in homes, florists' shops and in bookshops that the garden bouquet is regaining favour.

The happiest resolution would be to learn to appreciate and to create the best of both worlds, East and West. When your garden or your wallet is full and you feel exuberant, bring in an armload of flowers and enjoy the colour and richness of a mass arrangement. In quieter seasons, treasure the rhythm and grace of a few branches and blossoms in a line arrangement.

Another solution, one which is a compromise and brings with it all the dangers of compromise, is to combine the two types and make a line-mass arrangement. I have seen some beautiful arrangements which fall into this category, but I have seen as many which do not quite come off. The problem is to keep the final result from looking like a mass arrangement which sticks out oddly at two or three places, or like a line arrangement which has got a bit cluttered and lost simplicity without achieving exuberance or richness.

The line-mass is one of the most popular forms of arrangement today. As

time goes on, we should learn to invest it more often with the best qualities of the two parent traditions from which it was hybridized. At their best, both Eastern and Western styles have tried to emphasize the natural beauty of flowers, so that there is a necessary point of departure when combining them if a happy marriage is to be achieved.

The first step in making an arrangement is setting the shape, and in doing this you also set the proportions. As in anything else, getting the first steps right saves a lot of trouble later.

For a line arrangement you set the primary, highest line first. As I mentioned earlier, the classic rule is that it should be approximately one and a half times the height of the container (or the width of a flat container). Next set the secondary line, two-thirds the height of the primary, and then the third, or Earth, line, two-thirds the length of the secondary. All three lines should appear to emerge from the base at the same point. In the most classic sort of Japanese arrangement, they generally stay together for 4–5 inches above the container. The point at which the three lines come together is called the 'focal point'. In Western line or in line-mass arrangements, this is where you need to place the largest or most dominant flowers in order to achieve stability and to give the eye a resting place in the design.

If you are just beginning to practise arranging, you may want to check your proportions with a ruler. Go ahead and do it the first few times if it reassures you, but at the same time make yourself really look at the total effect so that your eyes will begin to develop judgement in gauging good proportion. Remember that flowers have different weights visually. You can go much higher with a wispy branch than you can with a ruffly piece of stock or a heavy gladiolus, and still maintain balance and proportion.

Before you cut the stems of the flowers that will set the line, hold them away from you against the container and move them to let your eye judge the best height and angle. Then make your cut, remembering that it is easier to shorten a stem than to lengthen it. As your eyes really begin to 'see', you will gain assurance and speed. After a good deal of practice, you may find that an odd phenomenon has taken place: your hands have somehow absorbed knowledge from what your eyes and your mind told them, and they have developed an almost independent skill. I discovered this when, after working as a florist for four years, I suddenly lost a major part of my central vision. After

the initial shock was over, my fingers literally ached to work again. Since the man I worked for was exceedingly kind, he let me have a go at it. And my hands showed me they could do it. With some intial help in sorting out colour distinctions from a fellow arranger, I was able to make arrangements that were quite normal and saleable.

The rules for creating a mass arrangement are less rigid than those for a line arrangement, but the need to achieve shape and proportion remains. You can start at any point: masking arranging aids with greens (often wise when doing centrepieces), placing a special flower that you want to occupy a prominent or focal position, or outlining the shape and establishing the proportions by setting your longest, spiky flowers into place first. The last is the easiest and safest way to start. The rule of thumb is one and a half times the height of the container for standing arrangements, and one and a half times the diameter for horizontal ones but, again, learn to judge the visual weights of differing types and colours of flowers and to adjust accordingly. Use the same technique recommended for line ar-

rangements: hold the flower in place and have a good look before you cut the stem. The goal is to finish an arrangement, stand back and *not* to say, 'Good Lord, I've got an elephant sitting on a peanut' (or vice versa). Outlining with the taller pieces gives you a clearer picture of what is happening.

As you work on an arrangement, check it from all the angles from which it will be seen. A flower arrangement is not one-dimensional, like a photograph. It is three-dimensional and must have balance and depth. The process of achieving balance and depth starts when you set the first flowers, outlining shape and establishing proportion, and continues through the placing of the focal point in a line arrangement, or the flowers you want to feature in a mass arrangement, right to the positioning of the secondary flowers, foliage and 'fill'. Not only do you have to cut stems to different lengths so that the heads will not all be in one line as you look at the arrangement from the front, you also have to vary the angle at which you place them from the back to the front so that they will not all be in one plane when you look from the side.

The variety of stem lengths and texture adds interest to this arrangement of Queen Anne's lace, daisies, globe thistles, hosta foliage, ivy and field grasses.

If you are doing an all-round arrangement, turn it as you work. If it is a line arrangement or a one-faced mass which will go against a wall, check it from the sides. Make sure it neither looks plastered back flat nor as if it were about to topple forward. When you are working on a surface lower than the one on which an arrangement will be seen, bend down frequently to see what it will look like in place. For arrangements which will be above eye level, such as on a mantelpiece, remember the medieval sculptures and allow for foreshortening. Looking up at nothing but stems and the undersides of the flowers heads is not very interesting. Flowers whose heads droop naturally or whose stems twist downward can present problems in ordinary arrangements, but come in handy for this type. One trick, if you are working with arranging foam, is to cut the block so that it rises $\frac{1}{4}$ inch or so above the container edge. Then you can easily angle short-stemmed flowers down over the rim. Make sure the ends of the stems do not poke out of the top of the foam, however.

For centrepieces, too, you should bend down frequently to see what they will look like when people are seated. You may feel like a jack-in-the-box at first, but as you gain experience you will not need to do it so often. Your eyes and

fingers will begin to know the angles at which to place flowers.

The ideal situation is to work where the arrangement is to be placed. If you take the trouble to spread out a sheet of plastic, such as a cleaner's bag, under the container, you will not have to worry about where stem ends and bits of foliage fall and you will save time later clearing up.

Rules have been set down about the visual weight of colours and sizes and how to balance them in flower arrangements. Briefly, the principle is that dark and vivid colours weigh more than light ones and that large forms weigh more than small ones. Large dark flowers should therefore be placed low and centrally in an arrangement, while small pale ones should be placed higher and towards the edges. This sounds fine as a general guideline, but in practice it is not that simple. Slavish and unimaginative adherence to this rule can produce an arrangement which is not only dull, but even unbalanced. Judging the visual weight of flowers in relation to each other, to the container and to the background, and learning to place them in an arrangement so that they balance, is something for which you have to develop an eye. The same flowers used in different circumstances can present quite different problems. For example,

a few sprays of dark Persian lilac in a mixed arrangement against a light background have enormous weight. However, if you use a mass of the same lilac, particularly against a dark background, with light pink peonies or black, shocking and pale pink parrot tulips, the lightest colours will have the greatest contrast, drawing the eye first, and will need the most careful balancing.

As you work, vary the lengths to which you cut the stems of your flowers in order to achieve depth. When you have finished, your eye should be able to move in and out of the arrangement, rather than resting on a flat, dull surface. As always, there are exceptions to the rule. A flat-surfaced bunch of daisies can be a very pleasant sight. At the shop where I worked, we displayed daisies for sale by putting five or six 'wholesale' bunches (twenty-five to the bunch) in large white plastic flowerpots. On more than one occasion customers demanded to have them delivered 'as they were'. We laughed, of course. We could have given them a good deal more show for their money by arranging the flowers in a looser manner. But the customers were right. Those round flat bunches were somehow a perfect way to arrange crisp daisies. The same thing happened with forget-me-nots and pansies when we mounded them in lined baskets.

of a daffodil or the spur of a nasturtium or columbine until you look at it from the side. We learn from the Oriental schools that every part of a plant is worth studying. The way in which a flower head attaches to the stem is sometimes fascinating, and there is almost as much variety in the shape of sepals as in petals. Of course, it would look awkward to plant a flower facing backward, front and centre in an arrangement, but you can easily show profiles towards the sides, and as you work around toward the back you can let the rear view of a flower be glimpsed between the ones in front of it. Some of the Dutch and Flemish flower paintings show the interest of this to perfection. Remember to leave space between the flowers so that the flowers behind can show through.

Leaving space between flowers in all layers, but most especially in the outline, is terribly important. If you do not do this, the result is a squashed 'clutter rather than a graceful arrangement. The spaces between flowers and leaves are a real part of the composition of your arrangement. If they frighten you, try looking at them for themselves. See how

Generally, however, the most interesting arrangements are those in which you see one flower peeping at you from behind another, a third almost hidden down in the depths and a fourth springing past them to trail out perhaps even beyond the outline of the piece. This gives not only depth but a feeling of motion and life to an arrangement.

In the outer layers, place the flowers you want to feature because of their colour or shape, or because of some quality that gives interest or balance to your arrangement. Sink to a lower layer less special flowers or ones that might upset the balance of the arrangement if placed in the upper layer. The visual weight of a large gold chrysanthemum can be changed if a pale yellow spider chrysanthemum trails out above it, softening the effect of its size and brightness. The deepest layer is the ideal place for using flowers you might otherwise throw away. You can use a rubrum lily which has had a few petals broken off or a chrysanthemum which has started to shatter in such a way that their presence will be noticed, but not their imperfections.

Try not to have all your flowers facing straight forward or outward from an arrangement. The profiles of most flowers are as interesting as their front views. You do not really see the trumpet

Step-by step instructions for a line arrangement:
1. Prepare the foam base and set the primary line with a spray of broom gently bent into shape.
2. Outline the basic shape. Note that the anthuriums all appear to spring from one point.
3. Sprays of heavy magnolia leaves extend the secondary line, and outline and reinforce the anthuriums clustered at the focal point.
4. Spider chrysanthemums are used to fill in and add variety of shape, colour and texture.
5. A few sprays of podocarpus foliage are added to soften the outline and the arrangement is done.

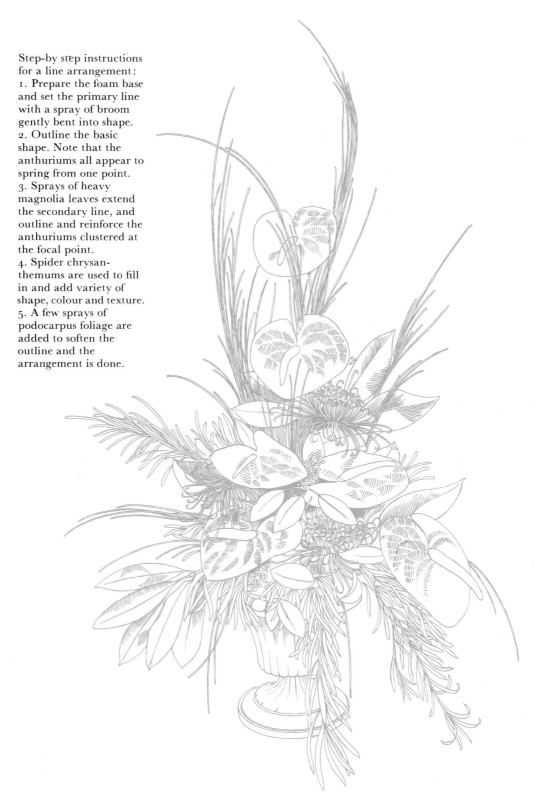

Right: this all-yellow arrangement shows how effective a monochromatic arrangement can be. The deep rich yellow of the 'heavier' flowers, the roses in the centre and the gladioli at the top, set the basic shape. In the foreground are the exotic multi-yellows of the smaller flowers, cymbidium orchids and clivia.

Left: wisteria, lavender-blue *Iris cristata*, white violets and moss in a bronze Chinese container. A late spring scene, inspired by the naturalistic Moribana arrangements of Japan.
Below: a formal centrepiece of roses (Woburn Abbey), lilies (Citronella), belladonna, delphinium and ivy in a silver Revere bowl.

A delicate arrangement of spring flowers in a bud vase. The longer sprays of foliage balance the container in a traditional 'fountain' shape.

interesting the outline of a space can be. As you get to the end of an arrangement, slow down and ask yourself, 'Is this flower really going to add anything?' If you are not sure whether a flower is needed or if it will be 'too much', you can try putting it in. It may work out beautifully and add just the richness you need. But if instead that particular flower bothers you when you have finished the arrangement and are giving it a final inspection, take it out. If you are afraid that pulling it out will destroy the arrangement, sneak a pair of scissors down along the stem to where it is hidden and cut.

On the other hand, the final inspection may reveal a genuine hole. One of the skills of arranging is knowing when to add and when to subtract. I think it is a good idea to set aside one or two flowers of the type you use in each layer, from the outline to the fill, and to save them until you think you have finished your arrangement. Unexpected gaps have an unfortunate way of turning up despite careful planning. Experienced arrangers as well as beginners find unforeseen holes in their designs. I have seen professionals in the best florists' shops go to get one more snapdragon for an otherwise finished piece. If you cannot go back to the shop or the garden for an extra flower, it is a life-saver to have a small reserve for repairs.

If you start to pull flowers out and try to rearrange to cover a gap, you will quickly end in disaster. For one thing, carefully established relationships between flowers will be lost. If you are working in plastic foam, too much poking about with heavy stems may destroy the stability of the block, and if you are working on a pinholder and depending on the flowers to support each other to some extent, you may cause a complete collapse. This is horribly frustrating and leads some people to think of flower arranging as a chore rather than the pleasure it can and should be. Thus, while a little quick adding or subtracting to correct obvious faults is fine, try to avoid being drawn into re-working. You are likely to lose your original freshness and perspective and create more problems than you solve. The flowers themselves will suffer from too much handling. Remember, if you have not quite achieved perfection this time, you can always try again with the next arrangement. That is one of the joys of the transitory art of flower arranging.

Up to this point I have mentioned colour only as a technical element in achieving balance, but of course it is a vital part of a good arrangement. The greatest joy in arranging for me is choosing the colours and watching them begin to work together as I arrange. Perfection of line, proportion and balance produced by great skill leave me cold if the colours say nothing; technically im-

perfect arrangements in which they whisper, shout or sing happily together give me great pleasure. This is a purely subjective reaction which I will not try to defend intellectually, but I believe reaction to colour is quite a personal matter. Psychologists have pointed out that different colours tend to induce different moods (blue is soothing, red exciting, yellow cheerful, etc.). Although this is generally true, people also form their own highly personal associations of ideas and moods with colours. For example, some women love pink, wear it, furnish whole rooms with it, while others cannot bear it.

That is what makes it so hard to give rules, or even advice, about colour. I have seen every law I have ever read or heard of on colour successfully broken. Each generation and nation seems to come up with its own set of rules about which colours go together and which do not. Loud and clashing colours were anathema to the Edwardians until the Russian ballet arrived with Leon Bakst's sets and costumes vibrating with purple, red, orange and gold.

When I first went to work as an apprentice florist, the chief assistant, an excellent arranger, informed me that no professional would ever combine pink and yellow. I wondered because I rather liked some shades of pink and yellow together, but he spoke with such authority that I was intimidated. Some years later I started arranging for an English lady who loved and ordered baskets of pink and yellow garden flowers. I had great fun finding the right shades of miniature carnations, roses, freesias, daisies, ranunculus, etc. The chief assistant passing my counter as I worked would occasionally snort, 'Pink and yellow?', but the expression on his face translated as, 'Ah, all right, it's not bad.'

Another combination which worked was what we came to call 'Dutch baskets'. I am not sure how the label came about. Perhaps it was because the first lady who bought them regularly had a Dutch surname, perhaps because the use of every colour in the rainbow and the wide variety of flowers was reminiscent of Dutch and Flemish paintings.

At this point it must seem as if I am saying anything goes in combining colours. But it is not quite as simple as that. Some combinations just do not work: they leave you feeling flat or irritated. Why? I think each colour in a combination has to have something to say to each of the others. The Dutch basket simply shouts, 'We're colour.' It may seem an unplanned mixture, but pastels and muted tones have to be rationed and placed carefully so that they contribute to the vibrancy rather than dominating and muting it. White should be handled as a rare strong colour like purple.

You can get a good colour conversation going between shades of pink and orange (African daisies are marvellous mixers in these combinations); they seem to be saying something about sunsets or dawn. If you throw in a few sprays of brown pompons the conversation stops cold. The same brown pompons put in with red, yellow and gold chrysanthemums will talk happily of dusty sunlight on autumn afternoons. Blue irises or delphiniums would be intruders in this conversation.

There are hundreds of theories, principles, rules and charts set down about the spectrum and which colours 'go together'. The problem is that, in trying to explain that in the right circumstances and chosen in the right shades any two colours will go together, the best of the theories become so complicated that I have never found them of much practical value. The best way to decide what colours to use in an arrangement is to hold the flowers together as you pick or buy them and see if an interesting conversation starts. Remember that bright and deep shades speak loudest, and apportion their numbers accordingly. This is a lot easier and, I believe, surer method than studying and memorizing colour charts.

Some very pretty arrangements can be made by using varying shades of one colour. Making monochromatic arrangements is a good way to get the feel of the mood and quality of different colours and their shades. I discovered this by accident at the shop where I worked. There was an order for centrepieces and arrangements for a dinner party at a hotel. We usually recommended yellow and white, the best colours for the decor of the banquet room, but this particular customer had specified all yellow. It sounded rather dull on paper. However, as I watched the chief assistant work on the order, I became fascinated. When he had finished, I said, 'That's really lovely.' He stepped back, surveyed the result and nodded. There were spires of snapdragons whose yellow was so bright that it might have come straight from a box of water colours. These contrasted with the very soft notes of yellow daisies, the pale yellow of small spray spider chrysanthemums and the deep, verging-on-orange trumpets of freesia. The whole thing sang about being yellow and how many ways there were to do it.

Most colours of flowers are effective used on their own, except perhaps white. The problem is that in the Western world we associate white flowers with weddings and funerals. This is a shame for they are so very beautiful. Looking at all white flowers occasionally seems somehow to rest, refreshen and sharpen my visual palate. The Orientals, who tend to avoid mixing bright colours which might detract from the fine linear quality of their arrangements, are not inhibited about using white alone. Indeed, they do so frequently. They celebrate New Year with white flowers, and the Chinese started forcing the paper-white narcissus for this purpose thousands of years ago.

These single-colour arrangements added to my awareness not only of colour, but also of the role played by the shape and texture of flowers. The interest of any arrangement, especially a monochromatic one, is increased if you use several different types of shape and texture. An arrangement consisting entirely of long spiky flowers tends to appear restless and unstable as your eye moves up and down it. One made of nothing but round compact flowers has the opposite effect, seeming too settled and self-contained. Irregular or complexly structured flowers, such as rubrum lilies, freesias, daffodils, irises or columbines, used together without the contrast of simple shapes, can be visually confusing.

The textures of flowers may not always be as obvious as their colours and shapes, but they are just as fascinating in their variety. I am not over-fond of gladioli, but I once almost hypnotized myself in the garden with the crystalline shimmer of one floret in the sunlight. Then there is the wonderful velvet of rose petals; it is hard to resist stroking them. I think one reason I love using Queen Anne's lace (wild carrot) with roses is the companionable difference in texture. You add a subtle interest to your arrangements if you use several different textures. Contrast shaggy petals with smooth ones, iridescent with matt, solid with airy.

However, do not carry the search for variety and interest so far that you lose sight of harmony. An arrangement should have an overall harmony of proportion, colour and feeling in the relationship of the flowers to each other and to the container and setting. We have already gone into proportion and colour. Harmony of feeling, like that of colour, is a matter that will be affected by personal association of ideas. I will set down my own general guidelines in case you find them useful. Harmony of feeling can be established by not mixing the seasons too much. (In other words, do not combine daffodils with chrysanthemums.) Avoid mixing very formal flowers with very informal ones: hybrid tea roses do not look comfortable in the company of black-eyed Susans. Try not to use exotic tropical flowers with temperate region garden ones: birds of paradise and sweet william do not bring out the best in each other.

There are as many exceptions to these rules of thumb as there are examples. Dutch arrangements obviously mix the seasons, although I try to stick to spring and summer and have a personal prejudice against including chrysanthemums. Daisies are quite an informal flower and yet seem at ease in the most elegant company. You just have to try various combinations and see what contributes to and what distracts from the feeling you are trying to establish.

When you finish an arrangement, hopefully you will not stand back and mutter, 'Shape, proportion, balance, depth, interest of colour, texture, harmony', but if these qualities are present, you will be able to say, 'I like it.'

This simple bunch of short-stemmed flowers would look dull if it were not for the great variety of flowers of different shapes and textures.

Spring

For the photographs taken in the Powell Room at the Metropolitan Museum, we chose flowers which would have been available in 1765. The result was this arrangement of red and purple anemones, white lilac, ranunculus, lilies, cornflowers, stock and strands of periwinkle.

Flowers always seem loveliest in their own season. With an apologetic bow to the horticulturists, nurserymen and florists who have worked long and skilfully to stretch and in some cases erase the boundaries of the seasons, chrysanthemums in May and irises in October bore me. As a florist I understand the commercial advantages of seasonless flowers, but as an arranger, professional and private, I am afraid they leave me cold.

The richest source of inspiration for flower arrangements is the observation of the moods, characteristics and colour schemes, both principal and secondary, which are woven into the changing tapestry of the seasons. These vary radically with geographic location, but they exist in some form almost anywhere there is plant life.

The first signs of spring arrive with raw winds, not much warmer than those of winter but bearing a sharp promise. The days grow gradually lighter and longer. The blue of the sky deepens above the scudding clouds and the sun strengthens. One morning a miracle occurs: the first crocus blooms and the earth begins to reflect the brightening sky in tiny pools and streams of gold crocus and blue scilla.

The earliest spring flowers are tiny, staying close to the ground to shelter from strong winds and driving rains. I cannot resist bringing some indoors to have close at hand when the skies close down and spring seems to be postponed again. However, because of their smallness, snowdrops, scilla, chionodoxa, *Iris reticulata*, and the later grape hyacinths,

pansies, violets, forget-me-nots and lily-of-the-valley present problems for an arranger. What do you put them in, how can you work with their slender, tender stems, and where do you place the small arrangements so they will not be overlooked?

Collecting vases can easily become a hobby, as I mentioned in the section on containers, and collecting miniature containers can be a fascinating sideline. Some of the antique ones are works of art. If you do not have an 'official' collection, a tour of the house, thinking small, should turn up things that will do nicely: empty perfume bottles that were too pretty to throw away, old silver salt cellars, finger bowls, ceramic mustard jars, ashtrays, even old inkwells.

If you are using a little bottle or something that does duty as a bud vase, you will not have much difficulty in making the flowers stay where you want them. All you need do is cut the right number of stems to varying lengths and add a few sprays of foliage to soften the effect. If the opening of your container is a relatively wide one, however, you may run into technical difficulties. The stems of most of the little flowers are so thin and fragile that the use of ordinary arranging aids, such as foam and chicken wire, is not practical. Very fine pinholders are some help, but without support at the top of the container they can prove frustrating.

One solution is to bunch the flowers and let them rest against the rim of the container. You can either do this in-

formally, gathering the flowers in one hand and twisting a rubber band (not too tightly) around all the stems at once, or you can bind a small central bunch with soft string or yarn which you continue winding around progressively larger circles of flowers until you reach the size you want. Tender flowers seem to last a little better in bunches since they protect each other from drying in the air.

You may want a looser, airier look. In that case try making a grid of narrow strips of arranging tape over the mouth of the container, secured by another strip over the ends at the edge. An alternative suggestion for containers with a lip is a single layer of gauze from a surgical pad, held in place by a rubber band. Preparations such as these may take a few minutes, but they save time in the actual arranging and make it a pleasure instead of an exasperating and fiddly chore.

Once you have made a small arrangement, where can you put it so that it will be noticed and enjoyed? Bedside, coffee and end tables, small surfaces near places where people stop to rest, are natural spots. Each home has its individual set of niches, shelves, desk corners, etc., which make good settings for small things. I do not like elaborate or unselective use of 'props' with flower arrangements of any size, and the creation of doll's house rooms around miniature arrangements bothers me very much. It seems to question the dignity of small flowers and the power their beauty gives them to draw attention to

themselves in a full-scale room.

Some scene-setting may be in order, however, if you want to give your arrangement a place of honour on a piece of furniture which is really too large in scale for it. In that case, the judicious use of a base, a small chest or a fine figurine, may help to make the flowers look more at home in their surroundings. An impeccable eye for proportion and your very best taste should guide you in this. If you have any doubts, let the flowers go it alone.

One of the prettiest ways to use tiny flowers in larger arrangements is to re-create their original environment for them. You can camouflage small containers in a miniature rockery built of moss and stones in a shallow dish and use the flowers cut, or you can plant them, bulbs or roots and all.

Before the scilla and the chionodoxa subside, the daffodils begin. There are likely to be a few warm days on which you can shed your heavy coat and really enjoy being outdoors. Even when the weather turns chill and grey again, you can look out of the window at clumps of daffodils and know that the falling rain is feeding the busy earth and will not hide the sun for long.

Daffodils do not last long indoors, but they are so prolific in the garden, inexpensive at the florist's and simple to arrange that it is no hardship to replace them more frequently than you would other flowers. They will last slightly longer if you cut them in the bud or when they are just opening.

You can use daffodils sparingly or *en masse*. If there are vacant containers with wide enough necks in your 'rockery', a few daffodils with their own foliage can bring it to life again. Or you can combine them with a budding branch and make a line arrangement in the Oriental manner. The advantage of this restrained use of daffodils is that you can really *see* the lovely shape of the golden trumpets which herald spring.

After the enforced economy of the long winter months, you may be thoroughly bored with restraint. In that case, bring in a basketful of daffodils and make sunburst bowls for dining and coffee tables. Take some foliage to go with the flowers. You will not want to rob your prize bulbs of the leaves which will help them store life for next year, but many gardens have a few patches of 'run-out' bulbs which produce nothing but foliage and can be raided with a clear conscience. Of the florists' daf-

fodils, only the large hothouse ones come with their own foliage. This is because the bulbs cannot be forced a second season. If you are buying the smaller, much less expensive, field-grown daffodils, choose the simplest leaves the florist will give or sell you to go with them. Nature had a sound aesthetic reason for combining the elaborate flower forms of daffodils, narcissi and hyacinths with plain, sword-shaped foliage.

A pinholder set in a cage with large openings, or combined with an open grid of florist's tape over the top of the container, is probably the easiest aid for arranging daffodils. Their stems tend to split and curl back if you try to force them into wire or foam. If you are using a few daffodils (or narcissi, hyacinths or anemones) in a mixed bouquet done in foam, keep a pencil handy to poke holes before pushing in these stems.

When you cut daffodil stems, they gush a slimy sap which should be wiped off so that it does not block the passage of water into the stems. Keep an old towel handy to wipe the stems and clean up any spilt sap. It can cause as sudden and dramatic a fall as any banana peel.

As the daffodils and the yellow fountains of forsythia fade, there is no pause in the garden. That is the exhilarating thing about spring – something is always happening. It is almost too much to take in all at once. The blue-and-gold colour scheme is replaced by a more varied one as green leaves unfurl along the branches, flowering trees and shrubs become clouds of rose and white, tulips appear in waves of white, palest pink to deep crimson, yellow to burnt orange and lavender to purple almost as dark as black. The scilla are replaced by lavender-blue grape hyacinths, and violets nestle between the flagstones. Something new appears each day.

Even if you do not have a garden, you need not be without the riches of spring. At this point in the year, florists begin to get local outdoor crops which are far less expensive than hothouse or imported ones. By the time the lilacs start, you ought to be able to indulge in an armload of flowers which will get all the effects of winter budgeting out of your system.

Tulips are one of the glories of spring, from the early low-growing *kaufmanniana* to the tall, elegant May-flowering varieties. Breeding them has fascinated horticulturists for centuries. Not only do they bloom in almost every colour of the spectrum, but in wonderful com-

binations: swirls, flecks, stripes, edgings and blends. A number of variations (parrot, lily-flowering, peony, etc.) have been bred from the characteristic tulip shape.

All this makes tulips irresistible to an arranger. They do present a few problems, however. Under certain conditions they have a tendency to collapse and hang limply over the edge of the container. If you have conditioned them properly and your arrangement is in a reasonably cool spot, this is unlikely to happen. If it does, remove the tulips and recondition them by cutting the stems, rolling them in a tube of newspaper for support and putting them in deep water in a cool spot. They should soon regain their crisp erectness.

Some varieties of tulip seem more prone to droop than others. The use of a copper container or the addition of a few copper coins to the water seems to help a little, but I believe the most important factor is temperature. At the shop, if we knew or suspected that tulips were going to an overheated place, we wired them. This may seem a very unaesthetic procedure to you, but if you are taking an arrangement to a friend in a hospital or to a crowded reception, you might consider doing it. People are far more likely to notice if tulips pull their dramatic fainting act than if they are discreetly wired.

Since my home is usually cooler than most, I am not much troubled by collapsing tulips, but there is another problem which I cannot escape. Cut tulips continue to grow in water. Also, like gerbera and anemones, they are extremely light-sensitive. This means you cannot arrange them once and be sure that you have finished. You are likely to discover the next day that the tulips in an arrangement have shot up an inch or so and moved from their original positions to point straight at the light.

A delicate arrangement of narcissus, forsythia and primroses grouped under a 'miniature' tree. The beautiful twisted branch is anchored to the base, an irregular slab of wood, by pieces of stone. The stem ends, tucked between the rocks, are wrapped in damp moss to help keep them fresh, but individual flowers could still easily be replaced.

The balance and shape of the arrangement is usually thoroughly disrupted, so you have to get out your knife and start cutting tulip stems and trying to coax the heads, now on crooked stems, into reasonable positions.

The only thing that will help keep the problem to a minimum is to place the arrangement as far as possible from any strong source of light, such as a lamp or bright window. Tulips also open and close in reaction to light. People's taste in this varies. If you want your tulips open, place them under a light; if you want them closed, keep them out of it.

The beauty of tulips certainly makes up for any extra work they may involve. They look well arranged by themselves with their own graceful foliage, either grouped in a single variety or in a whole rainbow of different ones. The rainbow is most dramatic if you have one or two black ones in it. A favourite combination of mine is red tulips with white narcissus, which is crisp and clean, the essence of spring. Another classic is red tulips and white candytuft. But the loveliest combination of all, I think, is lilac and parrot tulips, which usually bloom at the same time. Pink parrots, from pale to shocking, are wonderful with lavender lilac, and yellow parrots go beautifully with white, but then almost any flower goes well with lilac. By the time the tulips are past, the bearded irises and peonies come on to replace them, either on their own or with lilac.

Bearded irises are rarely sold commercially as cut flowers, but they do well in the home if you remember to snap off the fading heads and let the buds come on. Do not let the flowers touch a wall or any other surface for they stain dreadfully as they wither.

Peonies are one of the truly great flowers. I only wish their season were longer. They should be cut or bought as tight as possible, with the first coloured petals just showing. Do not be afraid that they will not open to full size if you take them at this stage; they will and you will have much longer to enjoy them. At the end of their span, peonies tend to shatter their blossoms. If you want to remove one from an otherwise good arrangement, avoid pulling it out by the stem or petals large and small will fly in all directions. Hold a waste-paper basket under the head and cut the stem where it will not show.

For the sake of convenience, I will draw a line here and say that spring ends with the peonies, before the roses get under way. Of course, Nature herself does not draw any lines in a garden, but continues weaving her tapestry. Who, except the astrologers, would dare say they knew the exact moment at which spring ends and summer begins?

Right: Bridal Pink roses, Queen Anne's lace, *speciosum rubrum* lilies and tuberoses in a Lalique bowl.
Below: white lilac, yellow tulips, gold iris and chartreuse euphorbia on a mantlepiece. The lower flowers have been aimed down more than they would be in a normal arrangement so that people seated in front of the fireplace will not look up and see only 'undersides'.

Summer

Summer in the garden, like spring, is not one season but several woven together. Nature, like a clever magician, distracts our attention from the vanishing of spring by bringing on to the scene the aristocratic perennials of early summer: roses, delphiniums, lilies, and a host of others.

The rose, traditionally the queen of flowers, is in its glory in the garden in June. It is quite a different creature from the roses sold all year round in flower shops. Florists' roses are bred for length and straightness of stem and for their attractiveness and durability in the bud stage in which they are sold. Some of the varieties are disappointingly flat-petalled when they open. I imagine the practice of valuing commercial roses by length comes from the Edwardian days when gallants of the wealthy class would pay small fortunes for walking-stick roses to catch a lady's attention.

I wish some florists would be a little more daring and experimental in their stocking of roses. If they were, I think they might find their market expanding as people became addicted to some of the wonderfully subtle variations of colour and shape found in roses.

Customers would have to do their part by not judging the freshness of a rose solely by its tightness. Tightness can be faked for a long period by peeling off the outer petals until the bud is a sad, soggy thing, like a middle-aged woman in debutante's dress. Some roses blow open quickly, but still last well. A fresh rose is one whose petals and foliage are crisp and firm.

Roses bloom in the garden until frost, but their greatest show is in the early summer before heat, drought and insects have had a chance to discourage them. Take advantage of the bounty and bring some indoors to arrange by themselves or in combination with other flowers. Roses should be cut late in the afternoon when they have stored in their cells the maximum amount of food manufactured by the plant during daylight hours. Single roses and those with relatively few petals should be cut in tight bud. 'Fat' roses (thirty-five to forty petals or more) should not be cut until the outer petals have begun to unfold, or their heavy heads may droop and fail to draw water. Experiment and experience will teach you the best stage to cut the varieties in your garden.

Cut the rose stem on a slant half an inch above the second full (five-leaflet) leaf with a very sharp implement, preferably a knife. Leave two good leaves on the stem end of the bush so that it has a good chance to produce more flowers. Never use any tool which will mash or tear the stem.

Condition your roses by plunging them in deep water and keeping them in a cool place for several hours before arranging. Never crush, peel or scrape rose stems for, despite their hardness, they are not like woody shrubs and the conducting vessels (xylem) should be left intact to enable them to draw water properly. Remove thorns below the waterline. This may seem a prickly nuisance, but if you skip it now you may regret it later when you start arranging

and the thorns tangle with each other, the foliage and your arranging medium. The quickest way to dethorn a rose is with downward flicks of a knife blade held parallel to the stem. You should also remove leaves and side shoots below the waterline. You may want to put these in water separately and use them in your arrangement. Some varieties have especially pretty leaves and, like most flowers, roses look their best arranged with their own foliage.

The arrangement you make will obviously be dictated largely by the roses you have available. An average small garden with one or two plants of a number of different varieties is most likely to yield a bouquet of red, yellow, pink, orange and white. There is nothing wrong with this. A bowl of mixed roses is as classic and charming an arrangement as you can make. Since they all belong to the same noble family you can get an interesting conversation going between them, despite (or perhaps because of) their colour differences.

You may have enough rose bushes (or sufficiently prolific ones) to be able to make arrangements of a single variety, of two, or of several different shades of one colour. If not, you might think about adding to your collection or of replacing varieties which you do not particularly like. You may actually start an arrangement of roses the day you receive the growers' catalogues. You know what colours go best in your home and how much space you have available in your garden. Modern catalogues with photography generally give detailed and accurate descriptions of foliage and the size and shape of flowers and bushes. Roses that will look well arranged together inside your house will probably, if some attention is paid to growth habits, look well growing together outside it.

If you have a period home you might try planting some of the old garden roses such as cabbage, moss (originally a sort of cabbage and very popular in Victorian days), damask (mentioned in Shakespeare and famous for its fragrance from medieval times), *R. alba* (ancient and not always white, despite its name), China, hybrid musk and Bourbon (first bred in the early nineteenth century). Most of the old roses have short blooming seasons (the last three I listed are exceptions), but if you are susceptible to their enormous charm you will find it well worthwhile giving them a place in your garden. They are not difficult to grow and are very hardy, persisting where modern hybrids sometimes falter.

If your space is limited, think about using climbers and ramblers which can be trained up walls, fences and posts. Some of them provide good cutting flowers. A delicate blossom pink, 'New Dawn', or a rose pink, 'Dr J. H. Nicholas', or 'Ritter von Barmstede', climbing behind a bed of blue delphinium spines and white Madonna lilies would give you a beautiful display in your garden and material for breathtaking arrangements. Or, if you like stronger colours, try the delphiniums

with bright orange Mid-Century lilies and a dark red climbing rose such as 'Crimson Glory', 'Don Juan' or 'Parkdirektor Riggers'. I like white daisies added to this arrangement to lighten it.

Both delphiniums and lilies present housekeeping problems. Delphiniums 'shatter' with age, although the hybrid strains are not so quick to do so as the simpler belladonna. I think having spines of sky and gentian blue in my home is well worth the minute it takes to dust under the arrangement, but that is a personal reaction. When the main stalks of delphiniums are cut the side shoots bloom. They are lovely in smaller arrangements and nosegays.

If delphiniums are cut back after flowering, and fed and watered during droughts, they will produce a second crop in late summer.

Lily pollen stains anything it touches, including flower petals. Remove the anthers (pollen sacs) from the stamens as the buds open, and the problem disappears. It is a shame since the prominent anthers are usually part of the drama of a lily's colour and shape, but if you have ever tried to remove the yellow-orange stain from a tablecloth or shirtsleeve, you will agree that it is the most practical thing to do.

Lily bulbs only bloom once in a season, but if you choose your varieties carefully you can have a succession of orange, yellow, pink and white lilies through August.

As the gentle warmth and the showers of early summer give way to the heat and

drought of July and August, the parade of grand perennials tapers off. The rich, soft colours of roses, Canterbury bells, lupins, sweet william, foxgloves, lavender, poppies and delphiniums are replaced by paintbox hues as the homely annuals take over and repay the trouble you took to plant them in the spring, producing flowers steadily and prolifically through the worst summer conditions. If you do not have a garden, you can still be grateful for the annuals. The ease with which they are grown makes them relatively cheap to buy in a flower shop.

Calendulas, zinnias, nasturtiums, cornflowers, marigolds, petunias, geraniums, snapdragons, dahlias, cosmos

A simple arrangement of *speciosum rubrum* lilies, following the naturally graceful curve of a piece of driftwood. The arrangement is supported by a base covered with soft green moss.

This shallow container gives a new look to a traditional arrangement of roses. The heavier open flowers are set in the centre, with longer-stemmed buds at the top and sides.

Left: marigolds, cosmos, parsley and watercress made a centrepiece of salad herbs and flowers for a summer meal on the terrace.

Right: red dahlias, pink lilies, salmon zinnias, cosmos, lavender and purple China asters in a pewter vase. The spiky 'fill' is hardy asters.

Below: never be afraid of using one flower on its own; it encourages people to really look at it in detail. The intricacy of the nasturtium flower and its delightful lily-pad leaves are shown off to advantage in this simple bowl, and the naturally trailing stems have been encouraged to curl over to show the flower head and its 'spur' from all angles.

A mass arrangement of
summer garden flowers
in a simple earthenware
container: delphiniums,
zinnias, dahlias, mari-
golds and nasturtiums.

and stock are as much a part of the plea-sure of summer as picnics, insect songs and seaside holidays. I know people who object to having arrangements of vivid annuals in their homes because they say they look hot. I understand their re-action, but I do not share it. The bril-liant pinks, oranges, yellows, reds, blues and purples of the annuals are crisp colours and make me feel less soggy. I suppose it is rather like eating curry in a hot climate. When I am doing one of these 'firecracker' arrangements, I do not use many white or pastel zinnias, snapdragons or petunias so that the effect of the clash will not be blurred. Daisies, with their sun-yellow centres, seem to work in all right. Their white is so clear that it can take on the force of a hue and lighten strong colours without diluting them.

Zinnias cut from the garden last quite a respectable time in the house, but those bought in flower shops wilt more quickly. I mention this hesitantly, since it is a puzzle to which I have not yet found the answer. The florist I worked for has noticed the same thing and we have discussed it a number of times, speculating that either growers left cutting too late (that would be odd), or the zinnias simply objected to travel, while far more fragile-seeming flowers revived beautifully after longer trips. Perhaps being children of summer heat and dryness, they cannot take the cool

damp atmosphere of a florist's, al-though most flowers thrive in it. One thing that is certain about zinnias is that the many-petalled ones last much better than the single. The hybrid varieties, such as the giant cactus and dahlia types and the smaller pumilla, produce fully double flowers more consistently than the standard varieties. Zinnias can be rather stiff when arranged by them-selves. It helps to soften them if you sac-rifice a branch or two of new growth with buds and smaller leaves. This is a good way to use up any 'singles' that may have developed. The more promi-nent the dark centre where the seeds develop, the less time a zinnia is likely to last.

Marigolds, small mirrors of the sum-mer sun, are not as difficult as zinnias to arrange gracefully. Their delicate foli-age and branched, often curved, habit of growth helps. The small French mari-golds almost literally arrange them-selves if you just provide them with an earthenware pot of the right size. The large American (Giant African) mari-golds lend themselves easily to line ar-rangements if you make use of the buds and half-open flowers which are found in abundance even in florist's bunches. Marigolds last well, but they tend to foul their water, so it is a good idea to check regularly any arrangement in which you use them. Marigold stems should be scraped, like those of asters

and chrysanthemums.

Snapdragons and larkspur give height to summer arrangements. Unfortu-nately, the latter, like its cousin the perennial delphinium, is a shedder. Petunias and nasturtiums can add a graceful trailing note. Petunias, so widely used as a bedding plant, may seem odd to suggest as a cut flower. The problem with them is that a blossom only lasts about a day. However, if you take the trouble to pluck off the withered flowers the buds will open along the sprays for several more days. There is nothing quite like the velvety depth of a dark purple petunia. Nasturtiums, too, are unique. They are fascinating in every part: bud, flower, leaf and seed. The trailing varieties will add interest to the bottom of a summer mass arrange-ment. As a centrepiece for a small lunch-eon, fill a basket with nasturtiums, watercress, parsley and any salad herbs you can get from your garden or grocer. Or you could make small nosegays of nasturtiums surrounded with their own lily-pad leaves and put one at each guest's place. About five geranium heads ringed with *Galax aphylla* leaves also make charming summer nosegays for bedside tables, breakfast trays or to wear.

Fields and roadsides are another source of summer sunshine for your home. This is the easiest season to obtain wild flowers, although it is still important to remember about trespassing and endangered species. Remember also to take some grass; handfuls of tall grass worked into a mass arrangement of field flowers not only add interest and lightness to the silhouette but give the arrangement a wonderfully natural feeling, like having a small corner of a meadow in your home. Some grasses seed or drop indoors, some stay beautifully intact. You will have to experiment with your local ones to discover which are which. Take a walk along a suburban or country road and see what you can find. This is particularly fascinating when you are on holiday in a different region. We often go to the seaside, and I am always amazed each time I see how many plants survive wind and salt and how wonderfully the colours of flowers and foliage are in harmony with the sea and sand.

I have already talked about choosing suitable containers for flowers so that your arrangements have a unity of style and feeling. The different seasons of summer illustrate this well, if you allow me to oversimplify for the sake of brevity and clarity. The aristocratic perennials need elegant vases of crystal, porcelain and silver in aesthetically simple or tastefully sophisticated designs. Most of the annuals look best in earthenware, pottery, wood, pewter and copper, which have a comfortable country look. Wild flowers tend to fall into the same category as annuals. There are exceptions, of course, such as Queen Anne's lace (wild carrot) which is just as at home with roses as it is with black-eyed Susans. And there is no need to put all your elegant containers away when the

annuals take over the garden. Some of them may be perfect for different sorts of summer arrangements: green ones and cool ones.

When I said earlier that I quite enjoy looking at hot-coloured annuals in the summer, I did not mean I liked them exclusively. Arrangements of green leaves of different shades and shapes, either alone or combined with a few white or pale flowers, make a change of pace. More than that, they can be an actual relief during the 'dog days', a sort of visual air-conditioning.

One of my favourite summer arrangements is a tall cut-glass vase holding sprays of hemlock branches, their black-green old needles outlined with featherings of chartreuse new growth, mixed with unripe snowballs (*Hydrangea paniculata*), still tapering in shape, with pale green florets edging the white. It is as refreshing to look at as having a fountain in the living room.

Green arrangements should be made with as much care and skill as flower ones. When you gather material for them, try to think of green as a colour, as exciting and full of shades and variations as any other. In a green arrangement, leaves are not just a background or accessory, they are the main feature. Choose them with an eye to pleasing contrasts and harmonies of shape, texture and colour. Green arrangements will repay the time you spend on them by lasting a very long time.

If you have a garden or woods, you will be able to find plenty of material. There should be evergreens, such as hemlocks, cedars, junipers, yews and pines; and broad-leaved evergreens,

such as rhododendrons, andromeda, box, azalea, magnolia, camellia and holly. Deciduous trees such as oak, beech, mountain ash and Japanese maple will provide you with lighter greens and interesting shapes. For airiness and trailing effects, hunt for ferns and vines such as clematis, wisteria, trumpet creeper and *Vinca minor*. A herb patch will yield delicate sprays of grey-green from rosemary, lavender, artemisia and santolina, as well as scented geraniums and verbena, gems in any small green arrangement. (Herbs, by the way, should not be seen as a hobby just for gardening cooks. They have many uses outside the pot.)

If you do not have a garden or wood which you can raid, head for your florist. Any good florist keeps a wide stock of cut leaves aside from those he gives away. You will have to pay for the better foliage, but they are an excellent investment for they wear like iron. Depending on seasonal, market and weather conditions, you should find eucalyptus, both flat and spiral forms of this grey-green, linament-scented leaf, pittosporum (flat rosettes of dark green and a variegated form light green edged with white), camellia, broom, cedar, box, myrtle, rhododendron and magnolia.

Green arrangements are good at any time of year, but in summer they provide an invaluable oasis in the heat. If they last so long that you no longer notice them, try a transformation. Add a few white or pastel flowers. Looking at pale yellow lilies among green leaves is almost as cooling as drinking a glass of lemonade.

A mixed bunch of
summer annuals,
including zinnias,
petunias, marigolds,
dahlias and black-eyed
Susans.

Autumn

The rich orange of chrysanthemums and Chinese lanterns (physalis) combined with the glossy green of camellia leaves make a dramatically effective arrangement. The plain vase is an ideal foil, reflecting the glow of the flowers.

Summer lingers well into September in my region. As the days grow cooler and clearer, the summer flowers take on renewed vigour. Roses which may produce sulkily in the heatwaves of July and August put on a show second only to their great display in June. Marigolds bloom, grow and set new buds with no intimation of their mortality. The early varieties of chrysanthemum which began flowering in August seem to me like guests which have arrived before the hour set for their reception. They mingle awkwardly with the summer flowers whose party is still in full swing.

Gradually, however, the scene changes. The dusty green of late summer begins to turn to gold. Seedpods abound along the roads and in the meadows. Light frosts kill the tenderest annuals and scarlet leaves appear on trees and vines. This is the hour of the chrysanthemums. They flame in the garden in clumps and sprays of red, bronze, yellow, white, lavender, pink and gold. Their earthy, spiced scent is an essential ingredient in the smell of autumn.

Chrysanthemums are such familiar friends, valued for their beauty and because they last so wonderfully as cut flowers, that it is easy to assume they are as traditional a part of our gardens as roses or daffodils. Actually this is not the case in Europe and America. The chrysanthemum was known and loved from time immemorial in China, where it symbolizes autumn, but it was only in the mid-eighteenth century that oriental chrysanthemums reached England, and then America. A few native

European varieties – feverfew, costmary and ox-eye daisy – had long been known, but their humble charm could hardly have prepared Europeans for the wonderful range of colour and form of Chinese chrysanthemums. Oddly enough it seems to have taken the beautiful, untemperamental newcomers almost a century to gain the popularity they deserved and have today.

Chrysanthemums are a desirable flower for florists to stock all year because once they are properly conditioned they will last ten days to two weeks, even under adverse conditions. This makes them less of a risk for a florist and also makes it easy for him to satisfy customers who demand flowers which 'must last'. They are the safest gift to buy for an acquaintance who lacks imagination and skill with flowers, but expects them to sit up and behave properly.

Another advantage of chrysanthemums is their range of size and shape. In 1910 R. F. Felton, master florist (By Royal Warrant to H. M. King Edward) and prestigious judge of flower competitions, wrote, 'There is no kind of floral decoration for which the Chrysanthemum, in one form or another, is not perfectly suited, as the flowers range in size from the tiny . . . to those gigantic blooms on stems a yard long . . .'

Despite the changes in fashion in the last 65 years, most modern American and British florists would agree with Mr Felton about chrysanthemums. The large exhibition types with incurved or reflexed petals still do their sturdy duty where mass display is needed, as it is in

churches, hotel lobbies and reception rooms. The small pompons appear as 'fill' in every conceivable sort of arrangement, unfortunately even those which are supposed to be 'spring bouquets'.

And therein lies the problem. Familiarity *does* tend to breed contempt. People who really notice the flowers around them can become sated with the constant sight of the commoner types of chrysanthemum. I admit that ten months out of the year they bore me silly. When October comes, however, I shake myself and remember that the workhorse of the florist's trade is actually a superbly beautiful flower with a season all its own in which it reigns supreme.

In the autumn, the standard yellow and white exhibition chrysanthemums and bunches of pompons which florists habitually stock are submerged in a flood of other colours and shapes and you can see the real versatility of the chrysanthemum. There are tiny yellow button chrysanthemums, large buttons of tan with red-dot centres, lavender with rose dots, pompons in white, lavender, pink, orchid and subtly graduated shades from palest yellow through gold, copper, bronze and crimson; lacey white Snowdrift and its brilliant yellow twin, Jack Straw; daisy chrysanthemums, small ones with many heads on a spray and large single ones of glowing autumn red; spoon chrysanthemums with cupped tips on their tubular petals; large thread-petalled types, such as Spider and Fuji, in white, lime, yellow, bronze, crimson and lavender and, of course, there are the large exhibition

chrysanthemums, some in fascinating two-toned colours, petals tan on the outside and red on the inside. And they have their characteristic spiced scent, which they seem to lack the rest of the year. It is not hard to become enthusiastic about chrysanthemums in their own season.

All chrysanthemums need the same conditioning. The skin should be scraped from the surface of the stem where it will be *below the waterline*. (Scrape above that line and you let in air instead of water and defeat your own purpose.) The end of the stem should be broken off roughly rather than given a sharp slice. After conditioning, if you shorten the stems as you arrange, repeat the process of scraping the part of the stem that will be below water. Thus treated, chrysanthemums can last two weeks.

The leaves of chrysanthemums, though pretty, do not last nearly as well as the flowers, so it is usually a good idea to strip most of them off and use some other sort of foliage when you arrange. Oak leaves look marvellous with the autumn shades of chrysanthemums. Later in the year, Snowdrift looks lovely and appropriate mixed with Christmas foliage.

Chrysanthemums are basically round in shape, but they have so many ways of achieving roundness that an arrangement made only of chrysanthemums need not lack variety and interest. For long shapes you can use spray types tapering out to a bud. (You may have to prune a bit to get them to do this gracefully; use the flowers you cut out somewhere else in the arrangement.) Fuji and Spider chrysanthemums are excellent in line arrangements. Their Oriental heritage is so obvious that it seems only natural to use them in this manner. They need not be confined to

it exclusively, however. A European mass arrangement can gain a note of lightness from their airy delicacy.

Chrysanthemums combine well with gleanings from the autumn countryside: grains, leaves, grasses and berries such as bittersweet and pyracantha. When using grains (wheat, barley, etc.) it is often more graceful to arrange them in clusters of twos and threes with the heads at slightly different levels, rather than sticking them in individually. Maple leaves with their wonderful colours are always tempting, but they dry and curl so quickly that I have never found a practical way to use them in arrangements. However, if you gather individual leaves and press them in a weighted phone book or between sheets of newspaper under a rug, you can use them around an informal Hallowe'en centrepiece, spreading them along the table in the manner in which flat ferns are used at formal banquets.

For a centrepiece for a Hallowe'en party, I like to hollow out a squat pumpkin, fit the opening with a container with Oasis taped in and fill it with oak leaves and small, bright chrysanthemums. For a children's party you can carve or paint a Jack O'Lantern's face on the pumpkin and add a few of the witch, ghost or scarecrow novelties which are sold everywhere at this season.

In North America, cornucopias are one of the traditional decorations for Thanksgiving. I find them difficult to use as centrepieces because there is not a great deal you can do to make the back of the horn interesting to the people seated there, but they are very effective on a sideboard or buffet table. If you want to use one with flowers, find a shallow bowl which will just fit inside the opening (the horn is horizontal and the bowl sits inside in a normal bottom-down position so that the rims of horn and bowl are at right angles to each other). Tape in a block of arranging foam which rises well above the edge of the bowl. Insert branches of oak or other autumn leaves at a downward angle so that they spill out of the horn in an irregular fan. Mask the bowl and foam with shorter pieces. Then add sprays of chrysanthemums, shortening the stems and bringing up the angle at which you set them as you get closer to the container. Grains mix beautifully with the flowers, and you can add fruit, such as grapes, if you wish. Even if you do an arrangement entirely of fruit or of fruit and grains, you may find it a good idea

to use the base of Oasis and the leaves. It is easier to pile fruit gracefully in one's mind's eye than it is in reality. Fasten some of the fruit by the stem to wooden picks with wire and tape; set the pick in a firm base and the fruit is far more likely to stay where you want it, rather than remaining awkwardly obedient to the law of gravity. This technique is useful not only for cornucopias but for other difficult containers.

Fruit and nuts make the most traditional Thanksgiving or Harvest festival centrepieces. They carry out the theme of the day: giving thanks for a good harvest. Besides, flowers were not commonly used as dining table decorations until the nineteenth century. To be traditional, however, you need not feel you have to limit yourself to apples, pears and grapes. People in the seventeenth and eighteenth centuries were at least as sophisticated about fruit as we are today. The pineapple was a symbol of hospitality, which is why one finds it represented so often in crewel embroidery and wood carvings of the seventeenth and eighteenth centuries. This tradition, plus its dramatic shape and subtle colouring, make it a grand king post around which to build a pyramid of fruit.

Above: chrysanthemums and oak leaves in a wooden grain container. *Below:* marigolds, asters, liatris and grapes in a pumpkin.

Dried flowers

Compared to the bright and varied tapestry woven by the preceding seasons, late autumn seems bleak and depressing. Once you eyes have become accustomed to the sudden bareness, however, you begin to notice treasures which would be overlooked in richer seasons: chocolate-brown spires of dock along the road and in the fields, the empty gothic niches of milkweed pods, tapered crimson velvet heads of sumac, spiny horse chestnut jackets and their polished fruit, clusters of open Rose of Sharon pods – very different from the blossoms the tree bears in summer, but almost as flower-like, in a quiet way. Queen Anne's lace (wild carrot) is beautiful in all its stages. After its white petals have fallen, the flower closes up into a scooped-out ball full of little, green, burr-like seeds. (It is this stage which earned it its nickname of bird's nest.) Then the seeds are shed and in late autumn the head turns brown and opens flat again with hundreds of empty seed stems arranged like clusters of tiny stars.

The treasures Nature leaves behind in November are dry and their beauty is quiet and sculptural compared to those of other seasons, but very real, nonetheless. Long ago people learned to gather them and use them to decorate their homes in place of the flowers which had vanished. From there it was an easy step for the more foresighted among them to learn to gather flowers which grew during the summer and which, when cut, dried almost intact. Stored carefully these 'everlastings' could be brought out later to add variety and colour to winter bouquets. In the old days a good housewife spent much of the summer stocking her pantry shelves with preserved fruits and vegetables, her cold cellar with root vegetables and her warm, dry attic or kitchen rafters with multi-purposed herbs. Among the bunches of herbs she would hang everlasting flowers: strawflowers, globe amaranth, statice and pearly everlasting, preparing to guard her family's spirits against winter's bleakness, just as she would their bodies against its famine.

Air-drying is the oldest means of preserving flowers, but as early as the seventeenth century it was discovered that flowers which collapsed and lost colour if they were left out in the air could be preserved if they were carefully covered in clean, dry sand which supported them

Ornamental gourds come in a great variety of shapes and colours.

intact until all moisture had evaporated. Sand-drying is still a good method for many flowers. In this century there has been a new development: the use of silica gel, an extremely absorbent form of silica sold in flower shops under several brand names. Flowers dry far more quickly in silica gel than in sand (two to eight days as opposed to one to three weeks), and the colours are brighter and clearer, although not always true to the original. Silica gel is much lighter than sand, so a higher percentage of success is achieved with very delicate or complex flowers which tend to suffer damage in the heavier medium.

Before you get involved with any method of flower preserving you should know that three things are absolutely necessary: space, time and patience.

The space must be dry, dark and warm, and you will need a good deal of it. Even for air-drying, you need more room than you might imagine. The flowers have to be tied in fairly small bunches and the bunches spaced out from each other when they are hung so that air can circulate while they are drying. Otherwise flowers will be squashed out of shape and at worst they may mildew. After the flowers are dry they are too brittle to be jammed together in a small space.

For the sand and silica gel methods you need even more room: room for boxes of sand and canisters of silica which are being stored, room for those which are in use and should not be moved around too much for fear of damaging the flowers inside them, room for flowers which have finished drying and must be stored carefully to avoid damage, and finally room in which you can prepare the flowers for drying and then arrange them. It can take weeks or even months of working off and on to

assemble the dry flowers you want for just one arrangement. And, quite simply, working with dry flowers tends to be messy. If you are forever tripping over storage containers or trying to spread out your work materials on a kitchen table and then clearing them away again, it can become frustrating. Obviously, this is not the perfect hobby for someone who lives in a small apartment and leads a busy life.

If, however, you have proper space available and know yourself to have the patience to wait to see the results of your labour, you may find it very rewarding to spend the time and effort necessary to create dry arrangements. The end product will be flowers which last for months or even years, but which are not artificial.

Set up your work area properly in the beginning, and you are likely to have more fun and less frustration later on. Dampness is the great enemy, whether you are drying, storing or displaying the flowers. It can cause them to 'wilt', and in extreme cases to collapse completely. Strong light will fade the colours. In the old days attics were ideal. In modern houses there is sometimes a little-used storage room which makes a reasonable substitute.

You will need a work bench or table with room to spread out, and a stool or chair the right height for it. There should be some means of hanging flowers upside down to air-dry (wires or clothes lines stretched across the ceiling, hooks in beams or rafters, whatever is either there or most practical to put up).

Flowers which are to be dried should be in perfect condition. Generally, they should be at the peak of their bloom and cut after the dew has dried but before the sun reaches its height. There should be no trace of moisture on the surface of

Right: reed mace, dock, grasses, iris pods, tansy, wheat, yarrow and strawflowers in an old wooden grain measure. Most of these can be found on a foraging trip in the countryside.

Left: a Thanksgiving centrepiece of fresh fruit, crowned with a pineapple, the symbol of hospitality.
Below: a Hallowe'en pumpkin decorated with a grotesque face and filled with chrysanthemums.

Sea holly
and
strawflowers.

the petals, but they should be crisp and filled with water inside so that they have their best form. If there is any suspicion of wilt or if they are going to have to wait until you can work with them, condition them just as you would flowers for a live arrangement. Do not bother drying flowers which are bruised or damaged by insects; imperfections are exaggerated in preserved flowers.

There are exceptions to picking flowers at the height of their bloom. You may want to dry some flowers, such as roses, in their bud stage for variety of form and colour. (Remember that a bud is much more compact and dense than an open bloom and therefore will take a longer time to dry thoroughly.) Some air-dried flowers, such as goldenrod, should be picked in the bud stage because they continue opening during the drying process. If picked in full bloom, they are more prone to shatter. Strawflowers and pearly everlastings also continue opening after they are hung up to dry. Your greatest chance of failure (i.e. disintegrating dry flowers) comes when you start with a flower which is already overblown. With experience will come a sixth sense about which flowers in your garden are perfect for gathering.

Air-drying is the simplest method of

preserving flowers and its results are the most stable. Air-dried flowers are less likely to react to moisture in the atmosphere and to sag or lose colour after they are placed in arrangements than are sand- or silica-dried flowers. Generally, all you have to do is strip the foliage from the stems, secure the flowers in not-too-large bunches (six to twelve flowers) with rubber bands, hook a wire through the rubber band and hang the flowers upside down. The use of rubber bands is important. Stems shrink as they dry and rubber bands contract, holding the bunch securely, whereas string and wire do not.

In some cases, such as strawflowers, the stems of air-dried flowers become too brittle or weak to hold the flowers when they dry and should be cut off about half an inch below the head and replaced by a wire. When wiring is necessary it should always be done *before* the flower is dried, no matter what method of drying is to be employed. If you have ever tried to wire flowers after they have been dried you will know that it is an exercise in frustration. Another important reason for wiring before and not after is that as the nub of the stem and the flower head dry they shrink down onto the wire, gripping it firmly.

Because of the shrinking and gripping process that goes on in drying it is not only unnecessary but undesirable to insert the wire too far into the flower head. As the flower shrinks, it may pull back over the wire, leaving it exposed. This is particularly unattractive in flat-faced flowers, such as daisies, so use a little less wire than you think is necessary. Experience will teach you how far to go. The exceptions to this rule are hollow-stemmed flowers, like zinnias, which cannot shrink onto the wire. With them you will have to poke the wire all the way through the face of the flower, make a small hairpin bend at the top and pull the wire back down, nestling the hook into the petals so that it is as hidden as possible.

If it has occurred to you that wire stems sticking out of your dry arrangement here and there are not going to be very attractive, you are right. For this reason, while you are gathering flowers to dry, gather some stems too. They should obviously be types which are strong and attractive when dried. Larkspur, day lily, delphinium and celosia are all good. Just strip off any foliage and side shoots and spread them out to dry. Then, when you are arranging,

you can use florist's corsage tape to seal a short piece of wire from the flower head to the top of a dried stem. The substitute stem should resemble the natural one in size and appearance.

Unfortunately, not all flowers air-dry. It would be lovely if they did, but if you want to save some of your favourite tulips, peonies or roses to look at in November, you will have to use silica gel or sand. Silica gel tends to produce very clear, vivid colours, not always true to the original shade of the flower. Any blue in a red or pink colour is likely to become exaggerated: bluish-red becomes purple, rose becomes mauve, etc. Using sand will give you a more muted effect, although you will also get shifts from the original hue.

There are differences in the method of using sand and silica gel. Weight, which makes sand more difficult to use for very delicate flowers, has already been mentioned. The other major difference stems from the fact that silica gel is absorbent and sand is not. This is the reason why silica works so much faster. It is also the reason why it must be stored and used in airtight containers so that it cannot absorb moisture from the atmosphere, and why flowers preserved in it must be 'timed' and checked to make sure they are not 'overdone'. If flowers are left in silica too long they may become excessively dehydrated and shrunken, and the edges of the petals scorched in appearance. It is impossible to give an exact formula for timing flowers in silica gel. A rough rule of thumb is that open, thin-petalled flowers such as forget-me-nots, daisies, violas, etc., may be dry in two days or so, while fleshier ones, like tulips and peonies, will take four or five days, and something as dense as a large, tightly closed rose bud may need more than a week.

Initially, silica gel is more expensive to buy than sand. Like sand, however, it can be re-used indefinitely, if you take a few simple steps to recondition it periodically. Silica gel contains blue granules which act as an index to the amount of moisture it has absorbed. When, after several usings, the blue granules begin to fade, place the silica in an *open* tin in a low (250°F) oven until the blue granules reappear. If you get seriously involved with flower drying as a hobby, you may find it more practical to ask your florist to order you a professional-size tin of silica gel rather than playing about with small kits.

Clean sand is easy and inexpensive to obtain from a number of commercial sources (florists, hardware stores, building or garden suppliers, etc.). You can dig your own for nothing, of course, but in that case you had better sift it to remove pebbles and heavy debris and then flood it with water several times to flush away dirt and light impurities. Since sand is non-absorbent, you will not need to dry it out, but you may want to resift it once in a while to remove broken bits of flowers and stems.

When using silica gel, and more especially when using the heavier sand, you will discover that some flowers, such as open roses or single daisy types, have a depressing tendency to lose petals or shatter completely. The loss of one or two petals is not a serious problem. You can replace them by dipping the base of a petal in a drop of transparent, fast-drying glue and setting it carefully back into position. If, however, you have repeated disasters with a delicate flower you want to preserve, try an ounce of prevention. Glue the petals to the calyx *before* you dry the flower. Apply a thin coat of glue just at the base of the back of the petals with a fine, firmly pointed watercolour brush. If the glue is too stiff to spread easily, dilute it with a drop or two of water. Leave the flower on its stem and replace it in water to prevent it from wilting until the glue has completely dried. Do not cut and wire it until you are ready to put it in the sand or silica gel. You may have to glue more than one row of petals on some flowers, such as open roses. Use your glue sparingly. It does not take a great deal to do the job, and lumps of it with bits of sand or silica adhering will spoil the natural appearance of the flower.

The technique for covering flowers is the same for sand and silica gel. The main thing to keep in mind is that you are trying to preserve the natural shape of the flower. The petals of a rose curve up and out from its heart and then curl over and down like the crest of a wave. If you simply poured cups of silica gel over the centre of the rose the delicate curves would be crushed and petals pushed out of position. When you uncovered it four or five days later, you would find a very squashed and dead-looking object. This is doubly true when heavy sand is used.

The trick is to bury the flower without flattening or displacing the petals. To do this, first lay a base of sand or silica an inch or so deep in the bottom of your container (use an open carton for sand, a tin or plastic box which can be tightly covered for silica gel). Level the base by shaking or tapping the container (as you would a cup of sugar or flour). Decide whether the flowers will maintain their shapes best during the covering process if you place them face-up (round, many-petalled or cup-shaped flowers), face down (flat-faced daisy flowers and small-flowered sprays) or horizontally (tall spikes). Wire the stems, and bend the wire up out of the way. Sink the stem of the flower into the sand or silica gel base. Make sure there is an inch of space between the outer petals and the sides of the container. In the case of flowers which you are drying in the downward position, place flat-faced ones gently on the level

Dried cow parsley.

desiccant, scoop a hollow to fit convex-faced ones and build a little supporting mound for concave-faced ones. In a gentle stream pour just enough sand or silica gel around, under and between the lower petals to hold the flower securely in place. You can use a cup or a can for pouring, but you will find you have the best and quickest control of your medium if you take a fistful and let it funnel through the crook of your little finger. The closer your hand is to your work the more control you will have over where the sand or silica goes. Repeat this process with other flowers until you have filled the container. Do not crowd too much. Flowers should be about one inch from each other and from the edge of the container.

When the layer of flowers is in place, you can begin to cover it. Keep a stream of sand or silica moving gently and steadily over and between flowers so that the level builds up evenly and a constant pressure is maintained inside and outside, above and below each petal. Watch like a hawk. Stop if you see a petal suddenly move out of place because pressure has forced it into an unseen air pocket. Lift the petal gently back into position and let the sand or silica flow into the pocket to support the petal. When covering spiky flowers in a horizontal position, do not just let them lie on the base or the lower side will be flattened. Lift the stem just enough so that the florets on the bottom hang in a natural position and hold it there until you have built a layer of sand or silica deep enough to support the stem. If you are doing more than one spray, or a particularly large one, you may find it saves effort to build a makeshift support for the stems. Three strips of cardboard notched at equal intervals to support stems at top, middle and bottom and wedged across the width of the container is one method.

An autumn harvest of Indian corn, pumpkins, gourds, wheat and frost-touched grape leaves on a seventeenth-century pewter charger.

When you have completely covered the flowers, rap the container gently so that the silica gel or sand settles into any unsuspected air pockets. Close the containers of silica gel and seal them with tape. If you have more than one or two boxes of flowers drying at one time, you really should work out a system for keeping track of the contents and when they will be ready.

Earlier I gave very rough estimates on the drying time of flowers. Size, compactness and stage of bloom all have to be considered. In using sand, which is open to the air, the weather is an additional factor. If it is persistently rainy or humid, flowers will obviously take longer to dry. With sand, however, timing is not critical. Flowers can stay in it indefinitely without damage.

Timing is essential with silica gel because over-exposure can cause damage. With experience you will learn to make educated guesses on how long a given flower should take. When the day for checking arrives, gently pour off enough silica to expose a few florets or parts of some petals. If the flowers are crisp and dry to the touch they are probably ready.

Continue to gently pour off the silica gel (or sand) into another container. You must be as delicate in this operation as you were in the covering one, because once the flowers dry they become brittle and will break easily. Avoid suddenly righting the container in the middle of the pouring process; the drying agent shifting back onto freed petals can cause damage. Never try to reach into the sand or silica gel and pull the flowers out.

Flowers dried in sand will emerge cleaner than those preserved in silica. Hold a sand-dried flower upside down and tap the stem very gently with a

pencil or paintbrush handle. Tilt it in various directions and repeat the operation. This should dispose of almost all the trapped sand. Stubborn particles which are wedged in or stuck to a bit of glue can be removed with a pin or toothpick.

Silica-dried flowers are coated with a residue which is more complicated to remove. It is vital to do this thoroughly, however, not only for appearance's sake, but also because the residue retains an absorbent property which will attract moisture from the atmosphere and may cause the flower to crumple or collapse in humid weather. In some cases, blowing and careful dusting with a soft watercolour brush will do the job. For more complexly structured flowers, with nooks and crannies you cannot reach, take a handful of sand in the same manner as you did for the covering process, using the curve of your little finger as the base of a funnel, and let a small stream trickle down onto the flower. Unlike the covering process, you now want the sand particles to bounce and scatter, taking the silica dust with them, so hold your hand well up, a foot or more above the flower. Keep moving the flower so that sand does not build up at any point and break a petal. Sand used for cleaning must be kept separate from sand used for other purposes since it becomes mixed with silica dust and is, therefore, partially absorbent.

If you are not ready to arrange and display your dry flowers, store them carefully. The easiest way I know to store dry flower heads on short wire stems is to stick them into a sheet of styrofoam fastened to the bottom of a cardboard carton. Do not crowd, then if you did not wire some flowers before

drying, do it now. Dry flowers should never be left lying on their petals. When the box is full, seal it in a plastic bag and label it. Tall sprays are more difficult. Place them loosely (not touching) in a vase the right height with a cup of silica gel in the bottom.

Foliage adds as much grace and variety of shape and texture to a dry arrangement as it does to a live one. Unfortunately, few flowers can be dried with their leaves intact, so you will have to replace them with other foliage, preserved separately.

Some leaves and ferns can be dried in silica gel or sand. This process retains the three-dimensional quality of the foliage, but, of course, it is as painstaking as drying the flowers themselves and the results are brittle and must be handled with great care. Use the same technique as for covering flowers in the horizontal position.

Two simpler methods for preserving foliage are pressing and the use of a glycerine solution. Pressing is suitable for flat branches and ferns. Just place them on several thicknesses of absorbent paper, such as newspaper, making sure that no two leaves are touching. If some of the leaves overlap, place several small sheets of paper between them. Cover with more sheets of newspaper. Quite a few layers can be dried in one pile. The top layer of paper should be weighted with something heavy, such as boards or large books. The leaves will be dry in one to three weeks, but the easiest way to store them is just to leave them where they are until you are ready to use them. The drawback of this method is that the leaves and branches are completely flat and two-dimensional. You will have to be clever and use some imagination as you arrange to keep this from being too obvious.

Glycerine is an excellent means of preserving broad-leafed evergreens, ivy, vinca, galax, yew and many other types of foliage. Combine three parts warm water with one part glycerine and mix well. Crush or slit the ends of the stems for 2–3 inches and place sprays in containers the right size to hold them easily without crushing. Fill the containers with glycerine solution to a level an inch or more above the crushed stem ends. Check periodically to make sure this level is maintained and add more of the solution when necessary.

As the glycerine is absorbed from the lowest leaves to the tip of the branch, colour changes will occur. It will take

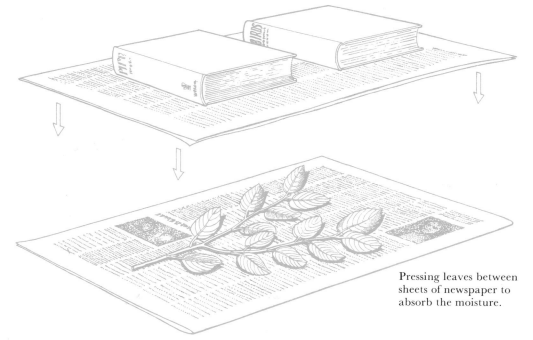

Pressing leaves between sheets of newspaper to absorb the moisture.

from four days to three weeks for absorption to be complete. When the tip of the branch has changed colour, remove it from the solution, wipe away any beads of glycerine which may have oozed out of the pores on the backs of the leaves and hang them upside down until you are ready to use them. The advantage of this method is that not only are the original structure and three-dimensionality of the leaves preserved, but they remain flexible and easy to work with. Glycerine-treated foliage lasts practically forever and can be stored and re-used year after year.

The difficulty with any method of preserving foliage is the change of colour. Autumn leaves present no problem. Cut just as they turn yellow, orange, red or russet, they retain their natural hues when pressed. The only thing you have to be careful about is not leaving them until too late. If you do, they will flutter off the branch when dried. Autumn foliage preserved in glycerine turns a warm brown which makes a natural and beautiful background for late summer and autumn flowers, particularly those in shades of yellow and red.

In an arrangement of pink tulips and spring flowers or June roses and delphiniums, however, autumn leaves would be a discordant note. The eye longs for familiar green. Unfortunately, lavishly as Nature uses green it is her least stable hue. You can preserve green foliage by any of the methods I have described, but it will not stay green long. Cut the foliage when it is fully mature. Unfurling spring leaves and tendrils are tempting, but they are delicate and wilt quickly, so you are not likely to have much luck with them. Put foliage which is to be pressed or covered in sand or silica gel in water first to make sure it is crisp and full. Wipe off any dust and trim damaged leaves. Foliage to be preserved in glycerine should be placed directly in the solution without any preconditioning in water.

Leaves will emerge green from sand, silica gel or paper. In glycerine some foliage will turn brown, but some remains green for a while, although usually a darker shade than it was originally. Placed in an arrangement, however, the chlorophyll which gives the green colour disintegrates rapidly when exposed to either natural or artificial light. The leaves will be left beige to dark brown, grey to almost black.

This may seem a dismal prospect at first, but it is no reason to abandon the

Teasels, honesty and Chinese lanterns.

variety of shape and texture leaves can add to a dry arrangement. There are two choices open to you. You can decide that green is absolutely necessary to make your arrangement pleasing and forget about being a purist. In that case, buy a can of spray paint in a flat finish and as quiet a shade of green as possible and spray away – with a light touch. On the other hand, you may decide that your arrangement is after all a dry, not a live one, and that being real itself it does not need to be painted to imitate another form of reality. Choose foliage of beige, brown or grey, whichever neutral is most flattering to the colours and mood of your arrangement, and use it sparingly. I usually find the second alternative works out more satisfactorily for me, but this is a matter of personal preference.

The basic principles for making a satisfying dry arrangement are the same as those for making a live one. Dry materials are much more brittle and delicate than live ones, however, and the less you have to handle them the better. Spend extra time planning what is to go where in you arrangement before you begin. It is worth it when you consider the time you have already spent preserving your flowers and the time you will have to enjoy your arrangement once it is done.

Styrofoam (for heavy, strong stems) and dry-arranging foam (for light, fragile ones) are the best bases I have found for arranging dry flowers. Since styrofoam, arranging foam and dry

flowers are all very light in weight, if your container is not a heavy one you may need to put sand or stones in the bottom to give your arrangement stability. Cut a piece of styrofoam or arranging foam the right size to wedge tightly in the opening of your container. Tape it for additional security. A base which does not wobble or shift can save you trouble later on. If you do not plan to make an arrangement packed so solidly with flowers and leaves that the base cannot be glimpsed through them, cover your arranging material with a piece of sheet moss. This natural and useful substance can be bought in rolls from a florist. Gently wring it out in water until it is damp and pliable. Trim a piece to fit over the base of your container and pin it in place with a few hairpin wires. Allow it to dry thoroughly before you begin to arrange.

Use corsage tape pulled tightly around and down to fasten wired flower heads to dry stems as close to their own as possible in size and appearance. This need not be done for all the flowers, but only for those which are going to stand out from the body of the arrangement.

Cut. the bottom of stems to a sharp point with a knife or clippers. If stem ends break off accidentally or prove too fragile to be stabbed into styrofoam, tape them to wooden florist's picks. This is the best method for handling clusters of small, thin-stemmed flowers, such as gypsophila (baby's breath) and rhodanthe. A note on gypsophila: to minimize it shattering and scattering dust when you try to work with it, dampen it first by sprinkling it with water as you would laundry you were preparing to iron. Once in place it will dry again very quickly. Do not let it come into contact with any silica-dried flowers while it is still damp.

Generally, when placing flowers in a dry arrangement try to work in layers. For a one-faced vertical arrangement, start with an outline toward the back and work steadily down from the top and in from the edges to the front. For an all-round vertical arrangement, work from the centre to the outer edges. For a horizontal arrangement, such as a centrepiece, place your outline and work from the lowest layer to the top one. In a live arrangement, the last flowers you usually put in are the 'fill' (small flowers which act to fill gaps and lighten the general effect). This is not the wisest way to proceed with a dry arrangement. Save your large, prize flowers until the very end. You can hold them in place to get a clear mental picture of where they will go, but do not set them in permanently until they will not be jostled by any further additions.

Preserving and arranging dry flowers may seem like a lot of work, and it is. If you have the time and patience for it, however, your reward is to capture what is normally a very fleeting beauty.

Right: dry heads of *Hydrangea paniculata* and silvery honesty, with dark brown accents of fertile Ostrich fern fronds and iris seed pods in a neo-classical urn.
Below: mountain ash berries and chrysanthemums in a pedestalled urn.

Winter

In general I prefer to use flowers in their own seasons but late winter is an exception. It is not just the simple, practical fact that there are not many seasonal winter flowers. There is a deep psychological need to escape the post-holiday blues and the prevailing drab chill of the weather.

We keep Christmas in our home for its traditional twelve days and relish it to the full. Unfortunately, this brings on an inevitable backlash. There is an old superstition that Christmas decorations left up after Twelfth Night bring bad luck, so on the sixth of January I set to undecorating with a vengeance. Everything goes, even the little boxwood trees which still look quite fresh. When the last ornament has been packed away, when the tree and wreaths have been dragged out and deposited forlornly on the rubbish pile, when the fallen needles and shrivelled berries have been swept up, a dreadful emptiness settles over the house.

Staring out of the window into the garden does not seem to help. Winter has its own beauties, less colourful and abundant than those of other seasons, but just as real if you are in the mood to look for them. For instance, you cannot see the architectural beauty of trees until they have lost their leaves. But somehow I find it hard to get into the right mood with Christmas just out of the house. Something has to be done to cheer things up.

My own prescription for curing post-holiday blues is literally to force spring into my home. Nothing lifts my spirits faster than the sight of buds swelling with life on bare branches, or a fat hyacinth poking up between spiky green leaves. They bring an immediate feeling that 'better days are coming'. Soon delicate petals will unfold on the branches and the hyacinth bud will stretch and open flowers to fill the room with the wonderful scent of spring.

Forcing some bulbs to bloom early is a relatively simple and inexpensive matter, considering the rewards involved. The easy bulbs include paper white and Soleil d'Or narcissus, French-Roman hyacinths, crocus and Dutch hyacinths which have been 'pre-cooled' or 'pre-conditioned' by the grower. They can be bought in the autumn, stored somewhere cool, such as the refrigerator, planted in successive crops, watered carefully and expected to bloom in roughly three weeks, depending on the variety and conditions. This can be done successfully almost anywhere, despite limitations of space and climate. Other bulbs which are not suitable for pre-conditioning, such as tulips, daffodils, grape hyacinths and *Iris reticulata*, require a good deal more time (up to four months), effort and space in a garden coldframe or an unheated cellar or garage.

The quick and easy method works perfectly well for pre-cooled lily-of-the-valley pips as well as spring bulbs. Buy bulbs and pips in the autumn at a garden centre or florist shop, or order them by mail from a reputable grower. Make sure they are specifically labelled pre-conditioned or pre-cooled for forcing.

The fatter the bulb the more it will cost and the larger the plant and flowers it will produce. In many cases this is a good investment. If, however, you have a mental picture of a bowlful of paper whites or hyacinths, you will find you get a more graceful grouping with a larger number of smaller bulbs in the container. No matter what size they are, the bulbs should be in good condition, with no bruises or soft spots and with the papery outer skins not stripped away by hard handling. You can store the bulbs in your refrigerator for quite a long time (up to two months) if you remember to keep them well ventilated and out of puddles of moisture which may rot them. Then you can plant them at intervals of ten days or more to ensure a succession of flowers during the late winter.

Bulbs can be forced in several different mediums. Since they are almost self-contained units, having stored their nourishment during the previous growing season, all they really need is water and something into which to sink their roots for stability. Pebbles and pearl chips are old favourites for paper whites, and hyacinth glasses for single hyacinths. This form of domestic hydroponics has its unique set of advantages and disadvantages. You have to watch the water level carefully. In the beginning the water should just touch the bottom of the bulb, enticing the roots to grow to reach it. Once they start growing you can let the level drop slightly. Never get carried away and surround the bulb itself with water or

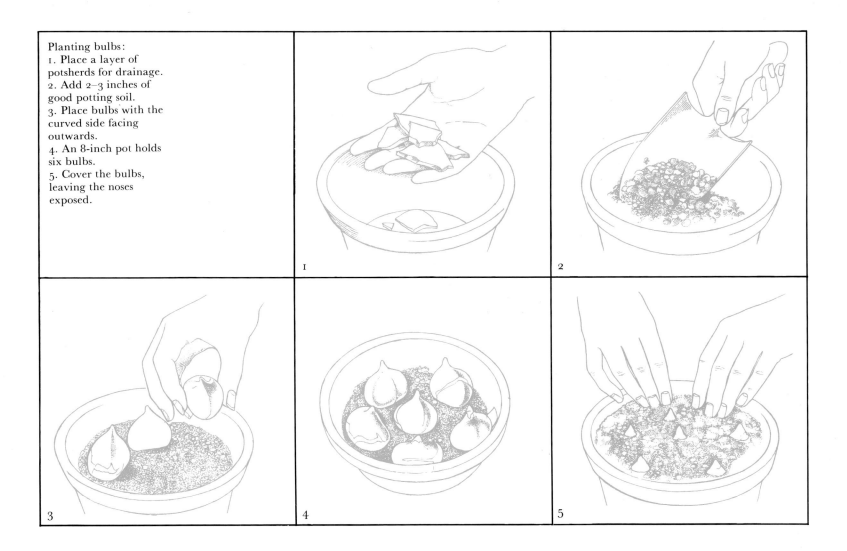

Planting bulbs:
1. Place a layer of potsherds for drainage.
2. Add 2–3 inches of good potting soil.
3. Place bulbs with the curved side facing outwards.
4. An 8-inch pot holds six bulbs.
5. Cover the bulbs, leaving the noses exposed.

1

2

3

4

5

Uncovering a pot to check its progress. Good root formation shows that the bulbs are ready to be brought into the light and forced into bloom.

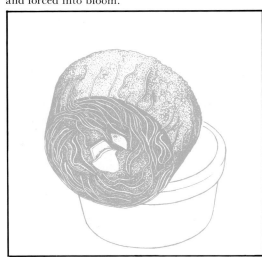

you will soon have a rotten mess on your hands.

The water level is easy to watch in hyacinth glasses. One of their beauties is that you can see the entire growth process. It makes a fascinating introduction for small children. (A quick aside: if you do this, have a short talk with the children before you turn them loose in the garden in spring. On two separate occasions I have been faced with looks of injured innocence and given the reasonable explanation, 'But I only wanted to see what the roots were doing.')

Water is not so easy to keep track of beneath pebbles. Bulbs planted in stones should be placed close together (gentle touching does no harm) on a base layer a couple of inches deep, so that their tops are not quite level with the rim of the container, and then surrounded with more pebbles for support, so that the pointed noses are left exposed. Periodically you will have to work an inquiring finger down among the stones to make sure that the water reaches just to the bottom of the bulbs.

It is important to keep the water fresh, although this may seem rather difficult. The addition of bits of charcoal in the beginning helps. Your nose will let you know quickly when a problem is developing. If it does, take the container to the sink and let a gentle stream from the tap run through the pebbles until the stale water is flushed out. Remember to pour off the excess.

An advantage of growing bulbs in pebbles and water is that you can use pretty containers. Narcissus and hyacinth look lovely in china bowls. I had always clung to the traditional belief that paper whites looked better massed in large clumps until recently I passed the window of an antique shop and stopped short at the sight of narcissus in full bloom singly and in twos and threes in small Chinese porcelain bowls. The bulbs had not pushed out of the pebbles (they look like Martians about to take off when they do this) and the plants did not appear too tall for the containers, as I would have imagined they might. In fact they looked charmingly and simply 'right'. That is the fun of flowers: some new way to create beauty always turns up when you least expect it.

Aside from water, bulbs can be forced in special fibres sold for the purpose, in peat moss and sand and in good, well-drained potting soil. For forced lily-of-the-valley pips, water alone produces disappointing results but a mixture of peat moss and sand is excellent. Incidentally, when you order pre-conditioned lily-of-the-valley, the pips arrive with a long, tangled mass of root growth which is awkward to handle in the relatively shallow containers in which the short plants look best, but the roots can be quite severely pruned without ill effect.

In most cases, I use potting soil for bulbs and pips, simply because it is obtainable in manageable quantities and easy to work with. If you want an attractive surface, you can always top-dress with a layer of pearl chips or sheet moss, or you can add a planting of grass seed and grow a tiny lawn around your sprouting bulbs or pips. As to containers, red clay and white plastic pots are both good and come in the proportionately shallower depths known as bulb pans.

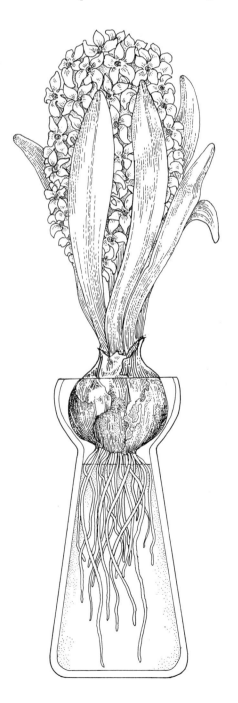

There is a perpetual debate on whether you should start your bulbs in the light or in the dark, once you have planted them. My mother puts hers in a closet to begin with while I put mine straight onto a cool sunless windowsill. We both get good results. My hunch is that plants started in good light are not quite so inclined to be leggy, but I cannot prove it scientifically. Experiment to find what works best in your home conditions. It is far more important to make sure that the bulbs are not exposed to too much heat which may hasten, but blast, their development. Watering is also of prime importance. Check the soil to make sure it is moist, but do not get over-anxious and water so much that it becomes sodden.

If you started your bulbs in the dark, bring them out when the shoots are an inch or two high. Do not be worried by the sickly yellow colour; they will rapidly turn green when the light gets at them. They should not be placed directly in the sun, however; they are not ready to stand it. In fact, I would rather not put forced bulbs in sunlight at any stage. It is not necessary to make them bloom and only seems to hasten their life cycle, which one should enjoy as long as possible. As your plants shoot up towards the light, give them a $180°$ turn from time to time so that their growth will be even.

You may enjoy the sight and smell of spring growing in your home so much after trying the 'quick and easy' bulbs that you want to experiment with more difficult ones, such as tulips and daffodils. If you have the right conditions, go ahead! They are worth the effort. For reasons of space, I cannot go into full detail here, but I will give you some

Left: a single hyacinth bulb forced in a hyacinth glass is fascinating to watch.
Right: forced narcissi bulbs bring a hint of spring in the bleak winter months. They look most effective massed together in a decorative china bowl.

Trees and shrubs which can be forced into bloom in the house.

Flowering

apple	crab apple	magnolia	pussy willow
apricot	flowering quince	peach	syringa
bridal wreath	forsythia*	pear	winter jasmine*
cherry	japonica	plum	witch hazel

Foliage

alder*	birch	Japanese maple	oak
barberry	grapevine	larch	sweet gum
beech	horse chestnut	mountain ash	

*suitable for early forcing

indication of the basic rules to follow.

Buy early-flowering, low-growing varieties, especially those described 'good for forcing'. Pot early in the autumn at the same time as you would plant outdoor bulbs and plant as you would the simpler bulbs: very close together in good potting soil, over a layer of potsherds for drainage, in bulb pans. The noses of large bulbs should be left exposed, those of small ones just covered.

Place the pots in a cold, but not freezing, place (35°–40°F) for a period of twelve or more weeks so that roots can grow. If kept indoors in a garage or cellar, the bulbs will need watering. If they are put outdoors in a trench or coldframe, no watering will be necessary in a normal season, but the pots will have to be covered with straw, sand, ashes, sawdust, peat moss or some material which *will not freeze hard*, and heavily mulched. If you simply dig the pots into the ground and cover them with earth, you may not get them out again until daffodils are blooming in the garden anyway.

After twelve weeks, tap the earthball out of a pot to see whether a good network of white roots has formed. If not, put the pot back. If roots have formed, it is time to bring the plant indoors and to begin to water and enjoy it. Keep bulbs in a cool (40°–55° F) place for three to four days before exposing them to increased heat and light. Water them regularly.

A frequent question asked about forced bulbs is 'Can I save them?' People become so fond of them in their eager, beautiful coming to life that the idea of discarding them when they have flowered is almost unbearable. Unfortunately, in most cases it is the only sensible thing to do. Once a bulb has been forced, it will not flower again indoors. The only exceptions are the hardy bulbs, such as Dutch hyacinths, which have been forced *in good soil* and close enough to their natural season so that they can be planted outdoors before the green leaves go and their cycle is complete. Plant these in the garden several inches below ground level, disturbing the roots as little as possible, with some bonemeal mixed in the soil under them, and hope for the best.

If I seem to have wandered from the subject of flower arranging, I apologize. Forced spring bulbs play such a vital role in the flower life of my home at a season when the garden is almost bare and florists' flowers are still expensive. Besides, you may find the skills you developed as an arranger coming into play as you choose types, quantities and colours of bulbs to plant for different 'crops', and later as you arrange the pots to make an effective display.

On a corner of my desk, where I normally keep a small arrangement of cut flowers, at this season I have a winter garden. Combined with two or three pots of bulbs (a medium-sized pan of narcissus, a single pink hyacinth and a small clump of lavender-striped crocus would be typical), are a fern and a half-hidden bud vase with a few freesias, ranunculas or tulips in it. The fern is a maidenhair which thrives amazingly in the light from the desk lamp and the not-too-distant windows. Its delicate fronds soften the sharp lines of the pots and the bulb leaves. The bud vase allows me to indulge my appetite for the rarer spring flowers without becoming too extravagant.

Even if you do not have the time or inclination to do your own growing, you can probably manage a winter garden. Most florists stock more forced bulbs after Christmas. Obviously it is not as cheap or as satisfying as doing it yourself. Large pans of tulips and daffodils are expensive, but one hyacinth, like a dozen daisies or a single rose, is among the best bargains to be found in a flower shop.

Spring bulbs are one great dispeller of winter gloom. Forced branches of blossoms and foliage are another. Somehow the term 'forced' traditionally applied to bulbs and branches brought to bloom indoors does not seem quite accurate, for, although we displace them from their natural season and outdoor setting, they spring to life and give us their beauty eagerly with no more application of force than the warmth of our home and the water they need.

I get my Twelfth Night branches, japonica (Japanese quince), from the florist, because where I live it is usually still a little too early to head for the garden, clippers in hand. The early branches sold by florists are not cheap, since they are obtained from nurserymen who shelter shrubs especially for this purpose, but they are a good investment as cut flowers go. Japonica, with its delicate white or shell-pink blossoms set on gnarled black branches, lasts for a good two weeks in my living room. Then there is an awkward stage when the flowers wither and some petals and pollen fall. If you are a terribly neat housewife (the sort who refuses to have delphinium in the house because it sheds), you may want to discard your japonica at this point. But if you can bear with it (a few flourishes with a vacuum cleaner hose and the mess vanishes), you will be rewarded. The little green shoots starting here and there along the branches unfold into candelabra of shiny, spring-like green leaves. This display, not a lush one but very cheerful, lasts well into February, by which time there is sure to be an early thaw and you can investigate what there is in the garden.

The hopeful days in January and February when the temperature goes above freezing and sap is rising, even though there is still a lot of winter ahead, is the perfect time to cut branches for forcing.

What you cut depends, of course, on what grows in your region, and on your personal preference. Forsythia, which turns into fountains of sun-yellow, and pussy willow with its soft grey 'kittens' mittens', hidden at first in hard brown shells, are understandable favourites. But do not limit yourself to the obvious. It is fascinating to watch many branches, not all of them flowering, come to life indoors: prunings from a grape vine, for example, or the unfurling fans on curving branches of horse chestnut.

When spring comes, everything happens at once and we hardly have time to notice all the individual miracles.

Watching forced branches in the quiet late days of winter gives us a chance to study a few of them.

Experiment to find what to cut and when. Just for reference, the list opposite shows some trees and shrubs which can be forced, some earlier than others.

Give cut branches the mashed stem treatment and place them in deep water. The amount of water branches require depends on the lushness of the flowers or foliage they produce and the number of new cells they have to supply. Forsythia tends to be thirstier than japonica (quince). The closer you cut to the normal flowering season, the faster the forcing process will be. You have to be patient with the earliest cuttings. Spraying with an atomizer definitely seems to help the process, if you can manage it without too much trouble or mess.

A note on dogwood: it forces well and is wonderful to work with in arrangements, but should be cut with discretion. Dogwood trees are one of the great beauties of the woods where they grow but they are not plentiful and should be protected. If you have trees on your own land whose shape will not be harmed by a little careful pruning, you can cut with a clear conscience. The branches sold in florists' shops are generally supplied by nurserymen who raise trees for this purpose.

When my Twelfth Night bunch of japonica has to give up its place in the tall vase, it can still be useful. The most interesting of the knobby branches cut to manageable proportions make perfect little 'trees' around which to create an Oriental arrangement. It is a good time of year to practise the economy of Oriental arranging. Add a half bunch of daffodils or narcissi, a few grape hyacinths from a florist or early snowdrops from the garden to a twisting branch set in a pinholder masked with moss in a shallow container, and you have another sort of spring garden to enjoy indoors.

Of course, there are other sorts of arrangement which will give you variety in winter. Carnations, both the large and miniature varieties, seem to be at their best in cool weather. Chincherinchee (Star-of-Bethlehem) wears like iron and is a good winter buy. For St Valentine's Day, I become completely sentimental and make a Victorian nosegay for a centrepiece. You can buy the paper lace holders at a florist's, cut out the centre, place it over a supporting ring of stiff leaves set in arranging foam and fill it with concentric rings of old-fashioned flowers, such as miniature roses, forget-me-nots, carnations and violets. Florists' stocks of flowers and leaves tend to be good at this time of year, and you can have as much fun as your budget allows. But basically it is my 'spring' gardens indoors which see me through the chill, grey days of winter until the true glory of spring bursts outside and the flower year begins again in earnest.

A Victorian nosegay for St Valentine's Day, using miniature roses and forget-me-nots.
Overleaf, left: a simple arrangement of apple blossom shows how an interestingly shaped branch can be used on its own to great effect. The pewter tankard gives a 'country cottage' feel to the Oriental shape and this arrangement would look charming in a chimney corner or on a small table.
Overleaf, right: Crocus chrysanthus 'Cream Beauty' planted in pebbles.

Christmas Decorations

Christmas is a season unto itself. It borrows some of its attributes from the natural seasons: from autumn's harvest of fruit comes inspiration for wreaths, garlanding and table decoration; from winter comes the theme of snow (even in areas where a white Christmas is a remote possibility), sleigh bells and evergreen boughs. Yet Christmas has its own identity distinct from the other seasons.

Christmas is a religious holiday, but non-Christians are drawn into it, just as the early Christians felt the influence of the Roman saturnalia and the northern pagan's use of mistletoe, holly and fir trees. Christmas celebrates childhood, friendship and family love with laughter and the giving of gifts. It has its own music, literature, food, drink and decorations.

Through all the traditions of Christmas, woven together from dozens of sources over the ages, runs the theme of merriment. It is a time for fun and fantasy, not for restraint. Nowhere is this more evident than in the way we decorate our homes. We bring whole trees indoors and trim them with angels and fairytale creatures. We can let ourselves go and combine ribbons, glitter, birds and toys with live plant material, which might be in questionable taste at any other time of year.

I have a few suggestions about things you can make to decorate your homes at Christmas. Some of these decorations, such as miniature boxwood Christmas trees, mistletoe balls, wreaths and garlanding, are expensive to buy in the shops, if they are available at all. The reason for this is not the materials, which are relatively inexpensive, but the amount of time and labour involved. Time and energy are precious commodities for everyone at Christmas, but the advantage of boxwood trees and mistletoe balls is that they can be made weeks in advance and kept fresh until you want them.

There are two types of boxwood available. 'American' boxwood, which bears pointed leaves on long, tapering branches, is the best for making miniature trees. 'English' boxwood has rounder leaves and a short, bushy growth. It is quicker and easier to work with when you are filling in mistletoe balls or rounded topiary decorations.

To make a boxwood tree, you will need a vase 2–3 inches deep with a footed or pedestal base, a whole block of the firmest arranging foam, arranging tape, a good armload of boxwood, a spray can of liquid plastic or glue and some gold glass glitter.

Soak the block of arranging foam thoroughly and set it on end in the vase. Fasten the block firmly in place with two bands of arranging tape at right angles to each other. For maximum security, use the tape full width where it sticks to the outside of the bowl for an inch, then just above the rim, fold it in half as it runs up to and across the top of the block. Pull the tape so taut that it bites into the edges of the block on top. If the tape slips on the bowl, heat the spot with a flame, press the tape down, run the flame briefly over the back of the the tape, press again and you should have a secure seal. Slice off the corners of the block between the tapes in wedges tapering out about three-quarters of the way down the block.

Now you are ready to 'set the tip'. This is the part of the operation which requires the most skill, so you may have to practise a bit before you get the hang of it. Choose a branch with as straight a tip as possible and break it off roughly 9–10 inches from the top. Break off any side branches which may stick out beyond the line of the narrow spire you want. If you have a good straight piece of boxwood which has too many side shoots at the tip, a little judicious pruning with fingernails or scissors can make it perfect. Sink the tip piece at least 2–3 inches into the middle of the top of the block. (If you have not quite centred the spot where the tapes cross, you will find this easier to do.)

Set in three or four secondary branches of boxwood, several inches shorter than the main piece, but slightly varied in length so that they do not all reach the same point on the main piece and create a clumpy ring. The secondary branches do not have to be as straight as the primary. If they curve, set the curve inward with the tip flat against the main piece and the bottom angled out from it. Repeat the operation with a circle of branches several inches shorter than the secondary ones. Use shorter sprigs for filling, almost covering the space on top of the angular cone of foam to create a graceful, slender spire for the top of your tree.

Next set the bottom, or skirt, of the

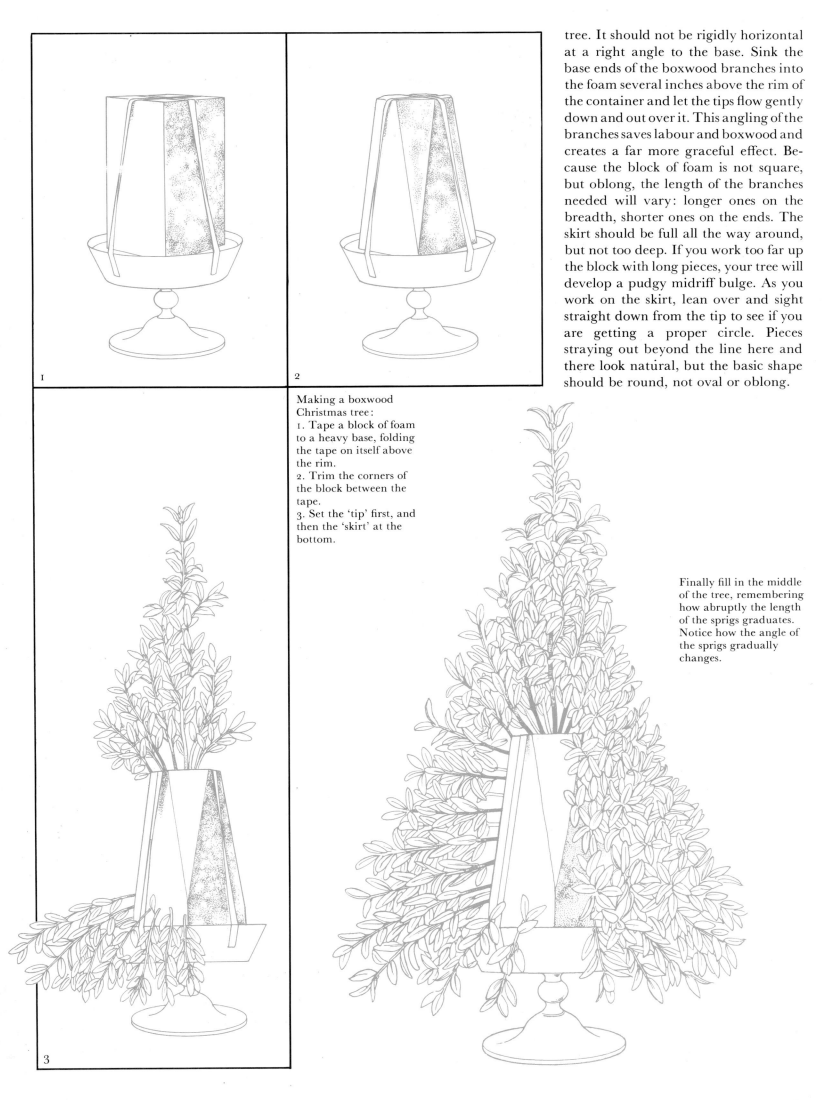

tree. It should not be rigidly horizontal at a right angle to the base. Sink the base ends of the boxwood branches into the foam several inches above the rim of the container and let the tips flow gently down and out over it. This angling of the branches saves labour and boxwood and creates a far more graceful effect. Because the block of foam is not square, but oblong, the length of the branches needed will vary: longer ones on the breadth, shorter ones on the ends. The skirt should be full all the way around, but not too deep. If you work too far up the block with long pieces, your tree will develop a pudgy midriff bulge. As you work on the skirt, lean over and sight straight down from the tip to see if you are getting a proper circle. Pieces straying out beyond the line here and there look natural, but the basic shape should be round, not oval or oblong.

Making a boxwood Christmas tree:
1. Tape a block of foam to a heavy base, folding the tape on itself above the rim.
2. Trim the corners of the block between the tape.
3. Set the 'tip' first, and then the 'skirt' at the bottom.

Finally fill in the middle of the tree, remembering how abruptly the length of the sprigs graduates. Notice how the angle of the sprigs gradually changes.

These little Christmas trees made of sprigs of fresh boxwood set in arranging foam will last for months. Ideas for decorating are almost limitless. The three shown here are Partridge-in-a-Pear-Tree, Birds in Snow and Santa Claus with Christmas parcels. A hint: when using artificial snow in a spray can, stand well back to get a natural feather effect. If you get too close the boxwood will be hidden and the result will look like a dripping ice-cream mould.

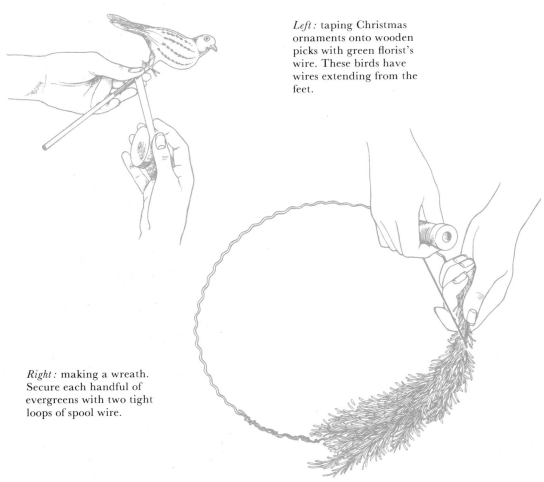

Left: taping Christmas ornaments onto wooden picks with green florist's wire. These birds have wires extending from the feet.

Right: making a wreath. Secure each handful of evergreens with two tight loops of spool wire.

Fill in between the skirt and the tip with boxwood pieces of varying length. The hardest thing for beginners to realize is how abruptly the length graduates from one spot to the next. The tip branches are quite long, while just below the flat top of the block you will need some sprigs hardly more than half an inch long. Until you get used to it, you may find it helpful to tie a string or ribbon around the tip and lead it in a graceful line down to the skirt. Keep it on the profile of the tree as you work, and if unsightly bulges appear beyond it, you will know you are breaking the sprays too long for certain levels. As you fill in, vary the angles at which you set the pieces so that you get a gentle graduation from the downward sweeping skirt to the perpendicular tip.

When you have finished you may want to give your tree a 'haircut' with a pair of scissors. Most trees need a little trimming, but the greater your skill in setting, the less cutting you will have to do and the more natural and beautiful your tree will be.

Spray liquid plastic or glitter glue liberally over the tree. This not only has the cosmetic effect of shining the dark green leaves, but also seals them from the air so that they stay fresh. Then, unless you are positively anti-tinsel at Christmas, add a light sprinkling of tiny gold glass 'glitters' (sold for

decorating packages) while the spray is still wet. The glitter should not be too heavy or obvious – just enough so that gleams of light are caught here and there in the branches of the tree.

Now you can have fun decorating. The ideas are limitless and you will create your own, but I cannot resist mentioning a few of my favourites: small gold angels with musical instruments, silver netting and milkweed pods painted blue inside and sprinkled with gold star sequins; white paper snowflakes with red bows; miniature fruit in rather formal swags and clusters; toy wooden soldiers; tiny cones sprayed gold with red ribbon; wool mice in nightcaps; gingerbread men, small candy canes, lollipops, peppermint balls and popcorn; or a natural, unglittered tree with a slender garland of tiny hemlock cones, Rose of Sharon seedpods, sprigs of rosemary and bows of the narrowest red velvet ribbon.

Secure your ornaments with narrow wire at the most convenient point and tape the wire firmly to wooden picks with stretchy green corsage tape. Then you can set the ornaments quickly in place with a minimum of fuss. Strands of miniature lights can be very effective. Tubular ribbon, sold for wrapping packages, makes excellent garlanding for the little trees.

The hanging of mistletoe is an older

custom in England and America than Christmas trees. Although it is surrounded by romantic legends of the Druids, Greeks and Germans, it is not a very pretty plant, at least not in the state it reaches us on the Christmas market. About the most attractive way you can hang it is as a pendant on a ball of glossy boxwood, decked with red ribbons.

To make such a mistletoe 'kissing' ball, you will need a well-soaked cube of heavy-duty arranging foam (roughly a 3-inch cube) folded securely into a cage made from a square piece of chicken wire. At the point where you close the cage by hooking the chicken wire onto itself, fasten a 'stem' of green pipe cleaner with a twisted loop at the outer end. Break a good supply of bushy English boxwood into 2–3-inch lengths. Then, either hanging the stem on a convenient nail or hook or holding it in your hand, insert sprigs of boxwood well into the cube of foam, circling it repeatedly until you have a full and, hopefully, well-rounded sphere. If you have a problem judging the roundness of your ball by eye, try silhouetting it against the opening of a 6–7-inch pot. Correct any obvious irregularities with a 'haircut'.

If you want to store the ball, dampen it thoroughly, put it in a plastic bag with the pipe-cleaner stem exposed and hang it in a cool place. It should be hung because if you lay it on its side it will become flattened. When you are ready to use it, spray it with plastic or glue and sprinkle lightly with glitter. Surround the prettiest piece of mistletoe you can find with a few loops and tails of narrow red ribbon, wire them firmly together, tape the wire ends onto a short wooden pick and insert the cluster directly into the centre of the bottom of the ball. Decorate with narrow bands or bows of ribbon, small glass balls, cones, sprigs of holly, or whatever suits your fancy.

Wreaths and garlands are both quite simple to make, though a bit hard on the hands. Although not set in foam like the boxwood trees and balls, they will stay quite fresh if stored in a cool place and kept damp. In any case, even if you work weeks ahead of Christmas, your home-made wreaths are likely to be a month fresher than commercial ones.

To make a wreath you will need a heavy wire ring, a spool of medium-weight wire and Christmas evergreens. Your florist will have the spool wire and

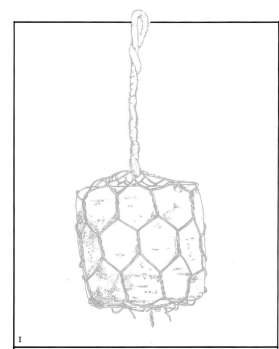

1

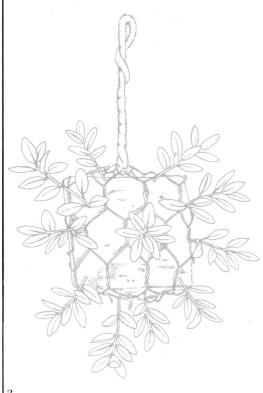

2

should have heavy wire rings in several diameters. If you are stuck, you could always hammer coathanger wire into a circle. The individuality of your wreath will depend on the foliage you choose. Balsam is traditional, of course, and I love it for its fragrance which is so much a part of Christmas. Boxwood alone makes a very tailored wreath, and the spruces are rich and full. Solid holly will make a wonderfully old-fashioned wreath but it dries quickly, so do not work with it ahead of time and do spray it with plastic or glitter glue to help keep it fresh. See what your garden or florist has to offer and mix or match evergreens to suit your own taste.

To start the wreath, hold the end of the spool wire flat against the ring with your hand, and with your working hand take several turns of the spool around the wire on the ring, pulling it as tight as you can so that the wire binds its own end firmly onto the frame and there is no danger of slipping or shifting. Place a handful of foliage on the frame at the point at which you have started the wire. The size of the first handful dictates the fullness of the wreath. You can have a slender, elegant one or a nice bushy one, as you choose. All subsequent handfuls should be about the same bulk as the first and

spaced evenly several inches apart, so that the loose tips of one handful cover the bound stem ends of the preceding handful, forming a fairly even outline.

If you are making a two-faced wreath, one which will hang in a window or glass door and be seen from both sides, the foliage should surround the ring completely. Arrange them in your hand like a small bouquet, with the 'good' sides facing outward, and then slip the ring into the middle. If your wreath is going to hang against a solid wall or door, you only need to cover the front and sides of the ring.

To bind the handfuls of evergreens onto the ring, spiral two loose turns of the spool wire down through the tips and stems of the branches and then bind the ends onto the ring with two good tight turns. If the first turns are too tight, you will get a bunchy, constrained look. Control the branches on the frame with your off hand and with your good hand work the spool of wire, drawing it from one side to the other, dropping it on your work surface, reaching under the wreath and pulling it across the back to the first side. It may sound awkward, but once you get the knack of it, you will find it very quick. Repeat the process – place a handful of foliage on the frame, two loose turns, two tight ones – until

Making a mistletoe ball:
1. Put a cube of foam in a 'cage' of chicken wire, with a pipe-cleaner stem looped at the end.
2. Set a circle of short bushy boxwood.
3. Continue filling in the circle until you have a ball.
The finished, decorated mistletoe ball is shown overleaf.

3

you complete the circle, and then bind the stem ends of the last bunch under the loose tips of the first. To finish off the wire, slip the spool through a loop around the ring ('tiering' it), pull tight, repeat once and cut. Add a wire for hanging, wire on cones or a ribbon and insert what decorations you like taped on wooden picks.

The technique for making garlands or roping Christmas evergreens is exactly the same as that for making wreaths, except that instead of using a heavy wire ring you bind your handfuls onto medium-weight, flexible cord. Garlanding tends to be more graceful and easier to decorate if it is 'all-round' rather than one-faced. Remember that the size of the handfuls of foliage dictates the thickness of the roping. Slender garlands are often attractive, and obviously more economical than bushy ones.

As Christmas draws closer, you may want to make centrepieces, baskets or arrangements of Christmas evergreens and . . . what? Red carnations are the only widely sold cut flowers which are a true Christmas red, but obedient to the law of supply and demand they are usually exorbitantly priced for the holiday. If you want to avoid straining an over-burdened budget, red berries make a less expensive substitute, or you can perch a few red cotton cardinals among the boughs or use clusters of red glass or silk balls. If the price is no object, but you do not want too much red and green, white freesia (normally just coming on the market) looks wonderfully elegant with variegated holly.

I hope your decorations will be so admired that you will find yourself wondering if you have time to make more as gifts for friends. I have found that even a simple basket of holly with a red-ribboned handle, which takes only ten minutes to make, gets an astonishingly cordial welcome. If flowers are your thing, and you have skill in your fingers, it is a nice thought to share them at Christmas.

Right: a mistletoe, or kissing, ball, an attractive way to use mistletoe.
Far right: variegated holly, incense cedar and wired ribbon decorate this wreath and matching garlands.

Appendix

A

Acacia (Mimosa) *Acacia dealbata*
Yellow; silvery fern-like foliage; early spring. Branches sold commercially (often as mimosa). Avoid cold and draughts and spray with water to help preserve fluffiness of flowers. Scrape and break woody stems.

Agapanthus *Agapanthus africanus*
Beautiful soft lavender-blue; in round clusters on 18–24-in stems; July–August. Lasts well in water, but tends to shed. Valuable to arrangers because blue is difficult to find.

Allium (Ornamental Onion)
Allium aflatunense
Violet; small tight ball on a 2-ft stem.
A. albopilosum: deep lilac; huge umbels (8–12 ins across) of star-shaped flowers with a metallic sheen on 2-ft stems.
A. azureum (*A. caerulum*): sky-blue small tight heads on 12–18-in stems.
A. giganteum: lilac; large ball on 4-ft stem.
A. moly: bright yellow; 3-in umbels, star-shaped flowers. May–July. Good, long-lasting cut flowers. Large varieties are dramatic in arrangements. Have the disadvantage of smelling of onion when cut. Change water frequently.

Alstroemeria (Lily of Peru)
Alstroemeria ligtu hybrids
White, pink, rose, red, lavender, yellow-orange, yellow zone and purple spots; trumpet-shaped flowers; pretty lance-like leaves. When fresh, heads have tight buds. Lasts one to two weeks.

Alum Root (see Coral Bells)

Anemone *Anemone*
A. coronaria (de Caen or St Brigid Anemone): brilliant red, lavender and purple with black centres; 2½-in blossoms.
A. hortensis: red, lavender, rosy-mauve and mauve, lavender, blue.
A. fulgens: scarlet, black-centred. March–May.
Anemones do not draw water well from heavy arranging foam. It is better to wedge a block of light foam into the top of a vase, with clear water beneath, make a path through it with a pencil and insert the stem through it into the water itself. When fresh and kept cool, lasts for five days.

Japanese Anemone *Anemone japonica*
White, pink, rose, red; single and double; August–October. Sharp cut and put in water promptly. Will last a week.

Antirrhinum (see Snapdragon)

Aquilegia (see Columbine)

Arum Lily (see Calla Lily)

Aster, China *Callistephus chinensis*
China asters include, nowadays, many varieties with large, fully double, round, white, cream, pink, rose, red, lavender, blue or purple flowers; August–September. For individual cultivars you should consult a seedsman's catalogue. Lasts two weeks in water. Scrape stems and break their ends.

Aster, Hardy (Michaelmas Daisy)
Aster
These are the true 'asters'. White, pink, red, lavender, blue, violet, purple with orange or yellow centres. These species are good for cutting:
A. amellus: lavender-blue, violet, pink, rose; large (2–3-in) single flowers; August–September.
A. cordifolius: white, lavender, small star-shaped flowers; October.
A. novae-belgii (New York Aster): white, cream, pink, rose, crimson, violet, mauve, lavender, blue; single and semi-double daisy flowers 9 ins–5 ft; summer through autumn.
Asters last extremely well. Scrape the woody stems and break ends.

Astilbe *Astilbe japonica*, etc. (incorrectly called Spiraea)
White, pink, red; feathery plumes; lasts several days cut from the garden.

Astrantia (Masterwort) *Astrantia major*
Greenish-pink; round. Lasts well when cut. The flowers have a formal old-fashioned charm and look like miniature Elizabethan ruffs.

B

Baby's Breath (see Gypsophila)

Balloon Flower (Chinese Bellflower) *Platycodon grandiflorum*
Rich blue, white and pink; balloon-shaped buds opening to bell flowers; July–August. Long-lasting, enormously charming cut flowers.

Bee Balm (Bergamot, Oswego Tea) *Monarda didyma*
Pink, scarlet, spiky crown-shaped blossoms, double-decked on square stems; July–September. Old-fashioned herb whose odd shape and fragrance creates interest. Long-lasting.

Bells of Ireland (Shellflower)
Molucella laevis
Insignificant white flowers with chartreuse-green shell-like calyces; August. Valuable in both line and mass arrangement. Lasts well.

Bergamot (see Bee Balm)

Black-eyed Susan (Yellow Daisy)
Rudbeckia hirta
Deep yellow rays surrounding a dark purplish-brown egg-shaped disc; 2–4-in daisy-shaped flowers; June–September.

Blanket Flower (see Gaillardia)

Blazing Star (see Liatris)

Bleeding Heart *Dicentra spectabilis*
Deep pink, heart-shaped flowers with a white pendant in sprays, graduating from blooms at base to buds at top; May–June.

Blue Lace Flower *Didiscus caeruleus*, syn. *Trachymene caerulea*.
Soft blue; round, flat 2-in clusters of tiny flowers resembling lace parasols; July–August. Watch for shedding when buying.

Boston Yellow Daisy (see Daisy)

Boxwood (Box) *Buxus*
Evergreen shrubs. Good filling when small-leaved foliage is needed. Excellent species are *B. sempervirens*, *B.s.* 'Rotundifolia' and *B.s.* 'Angustifolia'. Good for Christmas topiary arrangements.

Broom (Common Broom)
Cytisus scoparius
The long, narrow, green, easily-bent branches are excellent for modern line arrangements.

Buddleia (Butterfly Bush, Summer Lilac) *Buddleia davidii*
Mauve, purple, deep red, white; fragrant long spikes of small flowers; July–October.

Buttercup (see Ranunculus)

Butterfly Weed *Asclepias tuberosa*
Orange (yellow-orange to red-orange); tiny flowers in dense, flattish clusters; July–August.

C

Calendula (Pot Marigold)
Calendula officinalis
Shakespeare's 'Marygold'. Generally orange or rich yellow old-fashioned, homely flower, 3–4 ins in diameter, single or double. When buying, look at the back of the flower. The petals should be flat and true-colour, not curling into darkened spikes, shedding on being touched. Remove foliage below waterline. I prefer massing it by itself rather than mixing it with other flowers (except perhaps daisies).

Calico Bush (see Mountain Laurel)

Californian Poppy *Eschscholzia californica*
Cream, yellow, orange, red, pink; satiny, cup-shaped flowers; lacy blue-green foliage. Cut when in bud.

Calla Lily (Arum Lily)
Zantedeschia aethiopica, syn. *Richardia aethiopica*
White, large (8–10 ins long), funnel-shaped spathe with round edges flaring to a point surrounding a yellow spadix protruding from the centre; borne on a stout 3–5-ft stalk; glossy 2–3-ft leaves.
Z. elliottiana: bright yellow; tubular 6-in spathe.
Z. rehmanni: mauve-pink tube of spathe lined cream; dwarf. Widely available commercially. When buying there should be no blackening at edges or centre of the spathe or on the spadix. The spathe should be firm and smooth, not beginning to crumple. Calla lilies are not as popular as they once were, but they remain regal, dramatic flowers for line arrangements.

Camassia *Camassia*
Blue, lavender-blue, white; star-shaped flowers on 1–3-ft spikes; linear leaves.

Camellia *Camellia japonica*
White, pink, light-red, crimson, variegated; round flowers with curving, ruffled petals; single and double varieties. The dark green, glossy foliage is as valuable as the flowers to an arranger. Camellias are available commercially from late autumn into spring, their foliage all year round. Crack the woody branches at the bottom. An attractive centrepiece or bowl can be made with sprays of camellia foliage with blossoms nestled into it. In the spring you may be lucky enough to find some buds in the bunches of foliage. Even if you buy camellias which have been wired and cannot reach water, they will stay fresh for longer than you might expect if you sprinkle them with water and keep them reasonably cool. Check the petals for brown spots when buying.

Campanula *Campanula*
Campanula is a genus most of whose flowers are bell-shaped. Among the best known are:
C. medium (Canterbury Bell): white, blue, lavender, pink; flowers borne on tall (3–4-ft) branched stems; May–July.
C. medium 'Calycanthema' (Cup-and-Saucer): this variety differs from Canterbury Bell in that its calyx is coloured like the petals and stands out at the base of the flower like a saucer – hence the name; June.
C. persicifolia (Peach-leaved Bellflower): delicate blue; spikes to 3 ft, branched; June–July.
C. pyramidalis (Chimney Bellflower): pale blue; wide flowers on 4-ft spikes; July.
The tall spikes are not as useful for large arrangements as the spires of delphinium and foxglove, but the shape of the flowers adds interest and charm.

Canterbury Bell (see Campanula)

Candytuft *Iberis*
Annual and perennial species. The flowers of annual and perennial are alike: dozens of tiny flat petals arranged in compact racemes which lengthen with age. The annuals, erect, branching plants (12–18 ins), bloom all summer. The light green, somewhat lobed

leaves are rather like those of calendula, coarse and brittle. The stems are also brittle – beware when arranging. The perennials, 6–12 ins, bloom only in spring. Their lower stems are woody, the foliage fine, neat, dark-green.
I. amara: annual; white; fragrant large flowers.
I. sempervirens: perennial; white.
I. umbellata: annual; pink, violet, purple, red.
I. amara is available commercially. Its heavy lower stems should be peeled. The woody lower stems of perennial candytuft should be scraped. It is beautiful as a fill for spring arrangements.

Carnations and Miniature Carnations *Dianthus caryophyllus*
White, pale-pink through dusty pink, salmon, shocking pink to tomato-red, scarlet, crimson, cream, yellow, orange and variegated ('self', solid colour; 'flakes', striped with one other colour; 'bizarres', striped with two or more colours; 'picotees', petals edged or bordered with another colour); round, double flowers; narrow bluish-green foliage, pointed stems, spicy scent.
'Florist' or 'greenhouse' carnations (including the perpetual-flowering types) have flowers 3 ins in diameter with ruffled, edged petals borne on 16–24-in stems. Border carnations are bushier and more compact (12–14 ins high) than florists' carnations and bear flowers in profusion.
D. allwoodii: a hybrid cross between *D. plumarius* (Garden Pink) and *D. carophyllus*. Free-blooming, with a good, heavy texture.
Carnations and miniature carnations are available all year round commercially. When carnations are fresh, the head feels full and firm and there is no sign of darkening at the petal edges. When conditioning and arranging, take a sharp slanting cut above a stem joint.

Celosia *Celosia*
C. argentea 'Cristata' (Cockscomb): deep red, chartreuse, orange; fan-shaped or round heads of crumpled plush on strong 1½–2-ft stems. The large heads are awkward to use in most arrangements.
C. a. 'Plumosa' (Prince of Wales' Feathers, Prince's Plume): crimson, scarlet, salmon, gold; feathery plumes on 2–3-ft stems. Available commercially. Prince of Wales' Feathers is easier to combine with other flowers than Cockscomb. Both forms of celosia dry well.

Centaurea (see Cornflower *C. cyanus*; Sweet Sultan *C. moschata*)

Cherry Pie (see Heliotrope)

China Aster (see Aster, China)

Chinese Bellflower (see Balloon Flower)

Chionodoxa (Glory of the Snow) *Chionodoxa luciliae*
Light blue, white; star-shaped flowers marked with white in the centre of the petals; borne singly or in small clusters on 1–4-in stems. One of the earliest signs of spring in the garden; March and April. The flowers last only a few days in water, but at that time of year it is a pleasure to renew a miniature arrangement frequently.

Christmas Rose (see Hellebore)

Chrysanthemum *Chrysanthemum*
Chrysanthemums are one of the most popular, longest-lasting, most beautiful cut flowers. The colour range includes everything except blue and true purple; even green. Chrysanthemums are obtainable with blooms ranging in size from less than 1 in to 1 ft in diameter and in no less than nine forms. The principal of the latter are singles, which include the charming single Korean chrysanthemum; semi-double; anemone, with their anemone-type blooms; the neat rounded pompons, and their smaller counterparts, the buttons. Then there are the fascinating incurving chrysanthemums (football or exhibition) with petals rolling inwards; the reflexed with their outer petals curving back towards the stems; the spider or rayonnante with their thread-like petals; the quilled and tubular-petalled Fuji and the intriguing 'spoon' chrysanthemums with petals spoon-shaped at their ends. Some types are obtainable all the year round.
Conditioning: scrape stems and break, not slice, their ends.
See also: Daisy; Painted Daisy.

Cockscomb (see Celosia)

Columbine *Aquilegia*
A. alpina: deep blue; *A. caerulea*: sky blue and white; *A. canadensis*: red and yellow; *A. vulgaris*: blue. A rainbow of colours, some pastel, some bright; fairytale flowers with ruffled bonnets in front and spurs behind. The spurs are longer on the modern hybrids. The buds and flowers are borne gracefully on wiry, branching stems with attractive foliage. May–July. Rarely seen commercially as they are not good travellers, but last well cut from the garden.

Coral Bells (Alum Root) *Heuchera*
White, coral, crimson; tiny bells hung on a wiry stem 1–2 ft long; May, June and August. Adds a dainty note to arrangements if allowed to spring out airily.

Coreopsis (Tickweed) *Coreopsis*
Mainly gold, daisy-like flowers with broad, fringed ray petals and small tufty disks on long wiry stems. Annual (sometimes listed under the genus *Calliopsis*) and perennial forms. Coreopsis is a fine, long-stemmed cutting flower.

Cornflower (Bachelor's Button, Blue Bottle, etc.) *Centaurea cyanus*
Bright blue, white, pink, maroon; feathery-petalled, round flowers (1½ ins across), single and double varieties. When buying, make sure the colour is rich (flowers whiten with age). Wire if heads droop.

Cornus (see Dogwood)

Cosmos *Cosmos*
Round (3-in) flowers; July–August.
C. bipinnatus: the best-known cosmos in traditional colours: white, pink, lavender-pink, magenta; 3 ft or more.
C. diversifolius sanguineus (Black Cosmos): deep crimson; annual, to 18 ins.
C. sulphureus: yellow; annual; the new hybrids such as 'Bright Lights', 'Diablo', 'Goldcrest' and 'Sunset' are earlier, smaller plants with

smaller, sometimes semi-double flowers in shades of yellow, gold, orange, vermilion, red.
Cosmos are good cut flowers with long, graceful stems and attractive ferny foliage lasting five days or more. Occasionally available commercially in season.

Cup and Saucer (see Campanula)

D

Daffodil *Narcissus*
Daffodils are narcissi whose trumpet is as long or longer than the perianth. March–April. Everyone loves the solid yellow daffodils, but a flower arranger's scope is increased with some solid white, and some with yellow trumpet, white perianth, orange-yellow trumpet, white perianth, pink trumpet, pale yellow perianth. Cut when buds are showing colour and just beginning to open. The largest yellow hybrids (such as 'King Alfred') are available from December to April. They last better than the field-cut ones which are available in season, but are more expensive. Wipe off the slimy sap which oozes from the cut stem, before placing in water.

Dahlia *Dahlia*
Dahlias are very beautiful flowers that last about five days in water. They are obtainable in all colours, except pure blue and, perhaps, deep purple. The size of their flowers range from less than 2 to over 6 ins across. There are also several shapes: incurving, straight and recurved cactus, peony, semi-cactus, formal, informal and miniature decorative, ball, anemone, single, duplex, pompon and collarette. August–September. When buying, you should see that the petals are crisp.
Conditioning: sharp slanting cut (above a joint with hollowed stems of large varieties). A vertical slit in the stem between joints below water increases water flow.

Daisy
Chrysanthemum frutescens (Marguerite, Paris Daisy): white rays, yellow disc.
C. chrysaster (Boston Yellow Daisy): soft yellow rays, yellow disc.
Bellis perennis (English Daisy): white, pink, rose and crimson; small (2-in), round flowers, with many thin ray petals, some fully double, some semi-double showing a yellow disc; May–August. Dozens of ray and disc flowers of different genera are called 'daisy'. The wild flower most often meant is *C. leucanthemum* (Ox-eye Daisy): white rays, flat or indented yellow disc; blooms in fields, wasteland and along roads.
See also: Black-eyed Susan; Chrysanthemum; Doronicum (Leopard's Bane); Painted Daisy (Pyrethrum); Shasta Daisy.

Daphne *Daphne odora*
White rosy lavender; dense clusters of little petalled flowers; very fragrant; February–April; woody stems.

Day Lily *Hemerocallis*
Pale yellow, gold, orange, red, maroon. Trumpet-shaped flowers clustered on long (2–4-in) leafless stems; June–August. Modern lilies

have been hybridized from, among others, the species *H. flava*, *H. fulva* and *H. auriantiaca*.
Day lilies should not be rejected as cut flowers because each bloom only lasts a day. If you choose stalks with several buds, the withered flowers can easily be removed daily, so your arrangement keeps fresh for almost a week.

Delphinium (Annual) (Larkspur) *Delphinium*
White, cream, pink, rose, red, lavender, mauve, purple, blue. Similar to perennial delphinium, but the foliage is feathered; July onwards. Avoid buying when shedding petals excessively.

Delphinium (Perennial) *Delphinium*
Shades of blue, especially sky and gentian, white, and in the modern hybrid strains purple, mauve and pink. The 'Pacific Giant', 'Blackmore' and 'Langdon' Exhibition hybrids are good strains. The main spires of the giant hybrids can be used in large, impressive arrangements for special occasions, or standing alone, similar to spring-flowering branches. Secondary growth spikes are excellent for smaller arrangements. The perennial delphiniums have their main blooms in June. Delphiniums are available commercially (the giant hybrids mainly when in season, belladonnas sometimes forced). Delphiniums shed easily. When bought you should make sure that this is minimal.
Conditioning: small stems of delphiniums simply need a sharp cut. The hollow skins of giants might become air-locked when in water, so make a vertical slit in the stem, as for dahlias.

Dianthus *Dianthus*
I have listed the larger sorts as carnations and the smaller types and alpines as pinks:
D. allwoodii (see Carnation)
D. barbatus (see Sweet William)
D. caryophyllus (see Carnation)
D. plumarius, *D. alpinus* (see Pinks)

Dog's Tooth Violet (see Erythronium)

Dogwood *Cornus*
There are many species of dogwood (small trees and shrubs) which are valuable for their flowers in spring and early summer, and their berries (usually blue, white or red) and colourful foliage in autumn.
C. florida (Flowering Dogwood) is one of the loveliest species. In spring four showy, blunt-ended white bracts surround dense clusters of tiny green flowers, turning the branches into graceful white clouds. In autumn the foliage is a rich crimson and the fruit scarlet. Cut branches carefully with sharp pruning shears. Branches kept in the house in late February and March will bloom in three weeks. Conditioning: smash the bottom of the branches for several inches with a hammer.

Doronicum (Leopard's Bane) *Doronicum*
Yellow, daisy-like flowers on long stems; April–May. Lasts well, needs no scraping.

Dutchman's Breeches *Dicentra cucullaria*, *D. spectabilis*

White, tiny yellow pendant. The flowers look like little ($\frac{3}{4}$-in long) pantaloons hung upside down to dry on graceful 5–10-in stems; finely cut, attractive foliage.

E

Eremurus (Foxtail Lily) *Eremurus*
Star-shaped flowers; yellow, orange, white, pink, peach; 4–8 ft; May–July. Species: *E. bungei*, *E. himalaicus*, *E. robustus*.

Erythronium (Dog's Tooth Violet) *E. dens-canis*
White, pink, violet; 6 ins; April–May.

Euphorbia (Spurge) *Euphorbia*
Interesting fill or accent materials in arrangements are:
E. epithymoides: yellow bracts; April–May.
E. myrsinites: yellow bracts, grey-green leaves; March–April. Their milky sap must be kept in the stem after cutting, by singeing the stem end in a flame. (The sap is highly allergenic, sometimes poisonous. Wash your hands at once if you come in contact.)

F

Forget-me-not *Myosotis sylvatica*
Blue, white and pink; tiny flowers with five round petals and yellow 'eyes'; small light green leaves; April–mid-summer. Foliage and stems should be crisp; clusters should contain buds, not withered florets. Forget-me-nots last well if in clean water. Never let stems rest against sharp edges (such as a tin basket liner) or they will collapse.

Forsythia *Forsythia*
Intense yellow; small flowers like deeply cut bells borne before the leaves appear on strong, slender branches; March–April. Species are: *F. × intermedia*; *F. ovata*; *F. suspensa*; *F. viridissima*: bronze-purple leaves in autumn. Forsythia can be forced to bloom indoors if cut on sunny January or February days.

Foxglove *Digitalis*
White, cream, yellow, pink, rose, red, purple; thimble-shaped flowers, often prettily spotted inside, hanging to one side of a long spike on 1-ft (dwarf) – 6-ft stems; June–July.
D. ferruginea: rusty-red.
D. grandiflora: yellow, lightly veined brown inside.
D. lanata: off-white; odd flowers which add a quaint feeling to arrangements.
D. × mertonensis: crushed strawberry, rich spotting.
D. purpura: purplish, spotted flowers; grows wild in England and has naturalized occasionally in North America.
Of modern hybrids the following are good strains:
'Excelsior': full colour range; flowers borne all around spike, facing out so they show inner spotting; 5 ft.
'Shirley': white to deep rose; rich spotting; free-blooming; up to 7 ft.

Foxtail Lily (see Eremurus)

Freesia *Freesia*
White, cream, yellow (single and double varieties), gold, orange,
pink, pale and deep lavender; tubular bells; January–June. Commercially available almost all year round. The flowers should be firm, without any empty nubs at the base. Conditioning: sharp cut.

Fritillary *Fritillaria*
F. meleagris (Guinea-Hen Flower, Checkered Lily, Snakeshead Fritillary): chartreuse-yellow, reddish-brown, purple with deeper checked markings (var. *F. m. alba* is white); rather square, pendant bells with two or three six-pointed petals on leafy stems; April. Can add interest to an arrangement.
F. imperialis (Crown Imperial): red, orange, yellow; large bell-shaped flowers circling the top of a 3–4-ft stem surmounted by a crest of spiky foliage; April.

G

Gaillardia (Blanket Flower) *Gaillardia*
Yellow, orange-red, mahogany, petals often edged in a contrasting colour; ray and disc daisy-like flowers on long stems; toothed foliage.
G. grandiflora (syn. *aristata*): red, mahogany, edged yellow; 2-ft plants; mid-summer until frost. Cut 'tight', before fully opened.
G. pulchella: July until frost. 'Double Gaiety': mixed colours; 2 ft. 'Lollipop Dwarf': bi-colours and solids, fully double, ball-shaped, $2\frac{1}{2}$-in flowers on compact 10-in plant. 'Lorenziana': fully double globular heads.

Gayfeather (see Liatris)

Geranium (Zonal Pelargonium) *Pelargonium*
Double or single; orange-red, scarlet, pink, salmon, rose, magenta, white; velvety florets densely gathered in rounded heads on stiff stems; round, lobed foliage often with a darker zonal marking. The scented geraniums provide foliage which is attractive as well as perfumed:
P. capitatum 'Altar of Roses': light green, three-lobed ruffled leaves.
P. fragrans: nutmeg; trailing grey-green leaves.
P. odoratissimum: apple; light green leaves on vine-like branches.

Geum *Geum chiloense* var.
Yellow, orange, scarlet; round ruffled petals surrounding yellow stamens; May–September. Lasts several days when cut.

Gladiolus *Gladiolus*
An enormously hybridized genus; in all colours (including green, bi-colours and blended) except blue. Generally round, broad-petalled florets (plain, fluted, ruffled or toothed) are borne on stiff spikes 6 in–4 ft tall with sword-like foliage. May–October. Gladioli are commercially available all year round. Check to see that the lowest florets have not withered and been pulled off. Conditioning: sharp cut. Gladioli will last two weeks. Snap off withered florets.

Globe Thistle *Echinops*
Metallic-blue, round prickly heads on strong stems; June–August.

Glory of the Snow (see Chionodoxa)

Godetia *Godetia grandiflora*
White, pink, shocking pink, crimson with white zone at edges (also some orange shades); small poppy-shaped flowers clustered at tip of sturdy stem; July–September. Available commercially. Cut or buy with many buds, only one or two flowers open. Petals shed, but as buds keep opening head will remain attractive for a week. Scrape stem.

Goldenrod *Solidago*
This graceful yellow flower is excellent 'fill' for arrangements of summer flowers.

Grape Hyacinth *Muscari*
Blue, white; tiny bells hanging close together at the top of 4–8-in stems; March–May. Lasts well. Check to see that the bottom bells have not been peeled off, leaving a stubble of stemlets.

Grasses
Grasses look wonderful in informal arrangements of field flowers, daisies, annuals, etc.

Guinea-Hen Flower (see Fritillary)

Gypsophila (Baby's Breath) *Gypsophila*
White and pink tiny flowers borne on delicate-looking but sturdy many-branched stems.
G. elegans: white, pink, rose; single flowers.
G. paniculata: white and pink; more usually single, must be white when buying. Dries well.

H

Heliotrope (Cherry Pie) *Heliotropium peruvianum*
Lavender to deep violet, white; tiny flowers in dense clusters; vanilla fragrance; May–October. Conditioning: stem ends should be singed like those of euphorbia.

Hellebore *Helleborus*
H. niger (Christmas Rose): white (sometimes with a green or purple tinge) with prominent yellowish stamens, like large buttercups; December–March.
H. n. maximum: white tinged rose. This variety of Christmas Rose has flowers 3–5 ins across, sometimes more than one to a stem.
H. orientalis (Lenten Rose): purplish, green, pink, sometimes spotted; grows from 6–12 ins; February–April.
Hellebores are excellent cut flowers. Properly conditioned they will last two weeks. They lend themselves to subtle, interesting arrangements during the most barren season of the year.

Hemerocallis (see Day Lily)

Holly *Ilex aquifolium* (English Holly); *I. opaca* (American Holly)
Dark green, shiny leaves with large spiky toothed edges; red berries in winter.
I. aquifolium albo-marginata (Variegated Holly): cream or yellow edges; very effective in arrangements with dark ever-greens.
If you want to grow your own holly, remember there are male and female plants. Only the female plants bear berries, but you will need at least one male plant to fertilize them. So-called 'female plants' with smooth-edged leaves,
sometimes sold, are not always fertile. Holly dries and curls readily indoors. Spraying on both sides of leaves with plastic or glue helps.

Hyacinth *Hyacinthus orientalis*
White, cream, pink, rose, rose-red, pale and deep blue lavender, lilac-purple; fleshy bells with recurved petals massed on heavy spikes; spring. Top of spike should be still in bud when buying. Conditioning: wipe slimy sap from cut ends; do not keep in deep water. The large spikes of hyacinths can be awkward to use in mixed arrangements, although effective grouped at one end of a long shallow dish. Second spikes and spikes from garden bulbs that are past their prime, are more graceful, smaller and easier to arrange.

Hydrangea *Hydrangea paniculata* 'Grandiflora'
Creamy white; small flowers clustered on very large, tapered 'snowball' heads on long (2–4 in) stems. Form and colour are most interesting if picked when the tips of the 'snowballs' are still green. Scrape stems, break ends.

I

Iris *Iris*
Irises have flowers of almost every colour with three upright petals (standards) and three hanging ones (falls) and sword-like foliage. They grow from bulbs or rhizomes.
Bulb Iris:
I. danfordiae: lemon-yellow; 2 ins. Blooms very early.
I. reticulata: deep violet-blue; 6 ins. Blooms early.
Both of these only last two or three days in water so they need regular replacement in an arrangement.
Dutch, English and Spanish Iris:
English: blues and white; 10–14 ins; late June–July.
Spanish: white, yellow and blues, with orange-gold markings on falls; 1–2 ft; June.
Dutch: white, yellow, gold, bronze, lavender to deep violet blue; narrower standards and falls than the Spanish; 2–3 ft; early June.
Buy in bud or when just unfurling. Avoid open blooms with curling and darkening edges.
Rhizome Iris:
Bearded Iris: fuzzy, caterpillar-like growth on the falls; all colours, often different on falls and standards. Sometimes shaded, veined or with ruffled edges.
Tall bearded: 28–50 ins; May–early June.
Intermediate: 15–28 ins; May.
Dwarf: 10–15 ins; April–early May.
Miniature: under 10 ins.
The bearded irises, especially tall ones, are not popular with flower arrangers because their flowers are short-lived, they stain and their odour is sometimes unpleasant. You can effectively use them, however, if you choose branch stems carrying buds and remove the heads as they wither.
Crested Iris (the 'beard' is replaced by a notched ridge):
I. cristata: light blue, white; 4–5 in; late April–May.
I. tectorum (Roof Iris); light blue flecked lilac (var. *alba*: white); 12 ins; May–June.
Beardless Iris:

I. kaempferi (Japanese): white, pink, light blue to deep purple, often mottled, speckled or veined; large, flattened, often ruffled, flowers; 2 ft and taller; June–July. Good for Oriental arrangements.
I. sibirica (Siberian): light to deep blue, white, delicate butterfly flowers on 2–3-ft stems, slender grass-like foliage; June. A good cut flower.

J

Japanese Anemone (see Anemone)

Japonica (Japanese or Flowering Quince) *Chaenomeles speciosa*
White, pink, salmon, orange-red, deep red; small flowers with round petals and yellow stamens, usually appearing before foliage; March–April. Branches cut in late winter flower in the house in about three weeks. Buy in bud. The twisting, spiky branches and delicate blossoms are perfect material for Oriental line arrangements.

Jasmine *Jasminum officinale*
White; clusters of star-faced flowers; very fragrant; glossy compound foliage; June–October. Does not last well.

Jonquil *Narcissus jonquilla* (see Narcissus)
Yellow to orange; medium to short cupped, smallish flowers usually borne more than one to a stem; rounded sword foliage; stronger perfume than most narcissi. Wipe slime from cut stems. 'Baby Moon' is a pretty, delicate yellow, free-flowering hybrid.

K

Kalmia (see Mountain Laurel)

L

Larkspur (see Delphinium (annual))

Lavender *Lavandula spica* (formerly *officinalis*)
Lavender-blue; July–September.

Leopard's Bane (see Doronicum)

Liatris (Gayfeather, Blazing Star) *Liatris*
Light to deep orchid purple; round; borne on wand-like spikes.
L. pycnostachya: with 1½-ft long flower spikes.
L. spicata: Scrape stems. Extremely long-lasting.

Lilac *Syringa*
White, every shade from pale lavender through lilac to deep crimson purple; tiny flowers borne in large pyramidal panicles; heart-shaped leaves.
S. vulgaris (Common Lilac): stiff shrub to 20 ft; var. *alba*: white. Very fragrant.
French Lilac: hybrids of *S. vulgaris* with larger individual flowers (single and double) and heavier panicles. Generally not as fragrant as *S. vulgaris*.
S. persica (Persian Lilac): to 10 ft; slender graceful branches with showy blooms.
Available commercially (forced in winter, locally in season). Crush wood stems; remove lower foliage.

Lily *Lilium*
Large genus of stately charming plants of almost every colour except

true blue, often speckled and shaded; usually richly perfumed. The genus is too large for me to do more than list a few more easily obtainable species and strains:
L. auratum (Gold Band Lily): large ivory-white with yellow bands and dark speckles; fragrant; 6 ft; August–September. Imperial hybrid strains are impressive.
L. candidum (Madonna Lily): white; 4 ft; July.
L. chalcedonicum: Mid-Century hybrids (crosses of *L. tigrinum* and *L. hollandicum*): yellow to orange-red, dark-spotted; 3–5 ft; June–July.
Fiesta hybrids (crosses of *L. davidii* and *L. amabile*): pale yellow through orange to deep red; June–July.
Harlequin hybrids (crosses of *L. cernum* and *L. davidii*): ivory, pink, lilac, rose, salmon, violet, terra-corra-spotted; 5 ft; June–July.
L. henryi: yellow-orange; 6 ft; August–September.
L. martagon (Turk's-cap Lily): purple-red, also white and purple; 5 ft; July.
L. pardalinum (Leopard Lily): orange-red, crimson-spotted; 6 ft; July. The Bellingham hybrids of this species (yellow to orange-red) make wonderful cut flowers.
L. regale (Regal Lily): large white trumpets shaded yellow inside, streaked brown outside; 3–4 ft; July.
L. speciosum rubrum: rose, heavily spotted with carmine; 3–5 ft; autumn. Also *L. speciosum alba*: white.
L. tenuifolium (Coral Lily): scarlet; 1½–2 ft; June.
L. tigrinum (Tiger Lily): orange-red, maroon-black spots; 3–4 ft; July–September.
Buying lilies: see that there are buds and no empty flower stems, that foliage and flowers are crisp, and that the colour is true and not faded.
Conditioning: scrape heavy-stemmed types (Mid-Century and Easter Lilies) and remove anthers as flowers open because the pollen stains. See also: Day Lily; Fritillary (Checkered Lily); Eremurus (Foxtail Lily); Alstroemeria (Lily of Peru).

Lily-of-the-Valley *Convallaria majalis*
White (there is a pink species, but the white is lovelier and more popular). Small bells hung gracefully on one side of a slender, curving 3–8-in stem; pointed oblong leaves in pairs; exquisite fragrance. Lily-of-the-valley should be 'pulled', not cut, to get the best stem length. Available commercially, forced in winter, more cheaply in season. When buying, top buds should still be closed, with no signs of papering.

Love-in-a-Mist *Nigella damascena*
Shades of blue, also white and pink; very pretty round flowers with ruffs of lacy foliage on 12–18-in stems; June–August. Lasts well; occasionally available commercially.

Lupin *Lupinus*
Spikes with pea-shaped blossoms clustered along the upper portions; deeply cut, attractive palm-shaped foliage.

Russell hybrids (bred mainly from *L. arboreus* and *L. polyphyllus*): blue, mauve, violet, white, yellow, orange, red, salmon, pink; long dense flower spikes; 3–5 ft; May–July.
L. arboreus (Tree Lupin): yellow, gold, blue, lilac, white, mauve-pink. Cut tight, slit bottom of stems. Beautiful, but tends to shed.

M

Magnolia *Magnolia*
Flowers of a number of species of magnolia are available in the spring, commercially and from the garden. Buy or cut in bud as blossoms bruise easily.
M. grandiflora: large fragrant flowers, but not long-lasting. Large oval leaves, glossy green on the upper side, covered with brown felt-like down underneath. Blooms July–August. Foliage is extremely handsome and long-lasting in large arrangements. Available commercially. Crush heavy wood stem ends of both foliage and flower sprays.

Marguerite (see Daisy)

Marigold *Tagetes*
T. erecta (African Marigold): yellow, gold, orange; large (3–5-in) round heads, fully double with ruffled or spiky tubular rays; 1–3 ft; foliage has a pungent odour.
T. patula (French Marigold): yellow, gold, orange, dark red and reddish brown, single and double flowers; 18 ins; July until frost.
When bought, centre should be tight. Condition by scraping stems and removing leaves below water-line. Lasts at least one week. See also: Calendula.

Masterwort (see Astrantia)

Michaelmas Daisy (see Aster, Hardy)

Mignonette *Reseda odorata*
Stout, rounded spikes; moss green at the tip, tinged yellowish or rusty-red where the tiny flowers open around the tip; 12–18-in branching plants with rounded, oblong, rather brittle leaves. Available commercially; centre of spike should be tight with no sign of stripping of flowers at the base of the head and crisp foliage. Mignonette is valued mainly for its lovely fragrance, but I think its appearance is under-rated. While not at all spectacular, it can add great subtlety of colour and feeling to an old-fashioned arrangement. A ring of it in a nosegay, especially a yellow one, can make the whole effect 'come alive'.

Mimosa (see Acacia)

Mock Orange (see Philadelphus)

Mountain Laurel (Calico Bush) *Kalmia latifolia*
One of the most beautiful of American flowering evergreen shrubs. Glossy, dark green ovate leaves borne in clusters; pink to rose flowers with deeper markings; buds, borne in terminal clusters, have the shape of tiny ribbed lanterns; June. Both foliage and

flowers in their season are excellent for arranging. Available commercially. Crush woody stems; flowers long-lasting, but tend to shed.

N

Narcissus *Narcissus*
A large and lovely genus of spring-flowering bulbs which includes those commonly known as daffodils and jonquils. White, yellow, gold, some with pink, orange or orange-red shades in the central cup; mostly fragrant; spring. As a matter of interest, narcissi have been classified into eleven classes. If you want to know more, you should consult a good book or bulb grower's catalogue.
Buying: always tight in bud, never when petals show papery spots or curling edges.
Conditioning: cut stems, wipe off slimy sap. Plunge into water. Never arrange in plastic foam. Narcissus cannot be expected to last like chrysanthemums.

Nasturtium *Tropaeolum majus*
All the warm colours: cream through yellow, orange, red, crimson to mahogany; ruffled, bonnet-shaped flowers with five petals, the sepals fused into a single long spur behind; round leaves of fresh green with radiating veins; July–September.
'Gleam' strain: trailing types which will climb to 6 ft on trellises, or can clamber over banks or hang from windowboxes.
'Jewel' strain: dwarf, compact bushes 8–15 ins tall.
Pick when buds show colour and watch them unfold. Nasturtiums last only a few days as cut flowers, but they are one of my favourites.

Nemesia *Nemesia strumosa*
White, yellow, orange, red, pink, lavender; small, charming flowers borne loosely on 3-in spikes; fine linear foliage. Nemesia are small (to 18 ins) members of the snap-dragon family. Their stems are rather weak, but they look very gay in casual garden bouquets.

Nerine *Nerine bowdenii*
Deep pink; trumpet-shaped flowers with reflexed curly petals clustered at the top of 1-ft long stems; September. Available commercially autumn to spring. Lasts well with cleaning (buds open and fade in sequence).

Nicotiana (Flowering Tobacco Plant) *Nicotiana alata* syn. *affinis*
White, pink, rose, crimson, lime green; long-tubed, trumpet flowers with five-point star faces; lovely fragrance; sticky, hairy leaves and stems; 1–3-ft plants; July until first frost. Most nicotiana is evening-blooming (the 'Sensation mixed' strain stays open during the day). I have never had trouble with any type 'closing when used as a cut flower in the house.

O

Orchids
Expensive but long-lasting.

Ornamental Onion (see Allium)

Oswego Tea (see Bee Balm)

P

Painted Daisy (Pyrethrum, Painted Lady) *Chrysanthemum coccineum*
White, pink through crimson, lilac; single and double daisy-type flowers on long stems; May–June (second flowering September). Available at some florists close to normal season.

Pansy *Viola tricolor*
Modern pansies were developed in 1810 from *Viola tricolor* 'Hortensis' which is commonly called 'Heartsease', 'Tickle my Fancy' and 'Johnny Jumps Up'. April into summer. There are a few larger-flowered varieties: 'Engelmann's Giant', 'Majestic Giant', 'Swiss Giant', 'Oregon Giant' and 'Masterpiece'. 'Clear Crystals' are smaller in flower size, between a giant and a viola. Pansies do not last long when cut, but they can cheer a room up tremendously. Pick them just as they are opening, preferably as sprays with buds and leaves. When buying look for good texture – crisp and fresh. Do not use plastic foam.

Pelargonium (see Geranium)

Peony *Paeonia*
P. lactiflora (Chinese Peony): white, pink, rose, deep red and a few yellows; flowers up to 10 ins across; 3–4 ft; early summer. Foliage extremely useful for arranging. Chinese peony blossoms are classified as single, semi-double, Japanese, anemone and double.
P. officinalis (Old-fashioned Common Peony): single and double forms in white, pink and red; 2–3 ft; early summer. Tree Peonies: cream, yellow, white, pink, rose, crimson; single and double blossoms; May; graceful foliage 5–6 ft. Tree peonies are excellent for Oriental line arrangements.
Cut or buy peonies in tight bud. Conditioning: remove all foliage likely to be below waterline, cut stem end sharply and plunge deeply into water.

Periwinkle *Vinca minor*
Small, shiny, dark green, oval leaves; trailing, hardy plant. The graceful strands are useful when delicate trailing effects are needed. Small lavender-blue flowers; five squared petals; spring. The flowers are charming in nosegays, but do not last long.

Petunia *Petunia hybrida*
Every shade of pink to red, violet, lavender-blue to deep purple, white and soft yellows, solids, bi-colours and mixed colours; velvety trumpet-shaped flowers, single, double, some fringed or heavily ruffled: erect or trailing plants; June until frost. Not usually regarded as cut flowers, but worth trying. New buds continue to open as the flowers wither, when they can be picked off daily. The smaller, more prolific multiflora strains are better than the grandifloras, particularly when single.

Philadelphus (Mock Orange) *Philadelphus*
Blossoms white or white flushed pink, borne on loosely arching branches; sweetly scented; June–July; not very long-lasting. Crush woody stems.

Phlox *Phlox paniculata*
White, pink, magenta, salmon; small round flowers in large clustered heads on 2–4-ft stems; July–September. Rarely sold commercially because they do not last long and shed easily. Pick tight (when most flowers are buds) and you can enjoy the lovely scent, glowing colours and velvety texture for several days. Cut above joint in stem.

Pinks (Garden or Grass Pinks) *Dianthus plumarius*
White, shades of pink, rose, red, purple; parti-coloured, small single and double flowers with fringed petals, borne two or three to a stem on prolific plants; very fragrant, spicy; spring to mid-summer.
D. alpinus, D. allwoodii alpinus: large flowers on short stems; shiny, dark foliage.
D. arenarius: white; deeply cut petals; fragrant.
D. caesius (Cheddar Pink): rose.
D. chinensis (Annual Pink): red, lilac, white; 1-in flowers borne singly or loosely branched on 18-in plants. Not available commercially.

Pittosporum *Pittosporum tobira*
Lustrous, dark green, oval leaves up to 4 ins long; var. *variegatum* is lighter green with white margins. Cut branches are extremely decorative and long-lasting. Crush woody stem ends.

Polyanthus (see Primula)

Poppy *Papaver*
P. nudicaule (Iceland Poppy): white, yellow, orange, red, pink, salmon, champagne; 2–4-in flowers, with prominent yellow stamens; fragrant, grey foliage; May–June onwards.
P. orientale (Oriental Poppy): orange-red with black blotches at the base of each petal; also white, pink and deep red, with or without blotches; black stamens; 6–12-in flowers, single or double; May–June.
P. rhoeas (Corn Poppy, Field Poppy): red blotched black. Its progeny, Shirley Poppies, are white, pink, salmon rose and scarlet, without the dark centre; single and double, some with picotee edges.
Cut tight buds. Usually the night before blooming the drooping stem becomes erect; if possible, gather then. Condition by singeing and cut ends to seal in the sticky fluid. Plunge into warm water (100°F, 38°C). Poppies last reasonably well when cut.

Primrose (see Primula)

Primula (Primrose, Polyanthus) *Primula*
Very wide colour range: white, cream, grey, yellow, orange, red, salmon, pink, lavender, purple, violet, browns, with combinations, striped, blends, 'eyes'; dainty, velvety flowers; early to late spring.
P. auricula: full colour range.
P. denticulata ('Drumstick', or Himalayan Primrose): lilac, white, pink, red; ½-in flowers in ball-like clusters; early spring.
P. polyanthus (Polyanthus): full colour range.
P. vulgaris (English Primrose): typically soft yellow, but also pink, red, lavender and purple; fragrant.
Cut primula when clusters are about two-thirds open.

Prince of Wales' Feathers, Prince's Plume (see Celosia)

Pyrethrum (see Painted Daisy)

Pussy Willow *Salix discolor*
Silvery grey, furry catkins on spiky, sometimes branched, woody stems. Invaluable in line arrangements of spring bulbs. Leave in water until 'pussies' are fully developed, then remove or they will pollinate.

Q

Queen Anne's Lace *Daucus carota*
White; tiny flowers arranged in umbels (flat, round heads) 2–4 ins in diameter, giving the appearance of circles of fine lace; June–September in fields. Conditioning: sharp cut. Lasts well, but tends to shed with age.

Quince (see Japonica)

R

Ranunculus
Ranunculus is the name of the Buttercup genus. Beautiful and useful cut flowers.
R. asiaticus (Persian Buttercup. Turban Buttercup, Double Buttercup, etc.): shades of yellow, gold, orange, red, rose, pink, white and picotee mixtures; 2–4-in massed round flowers, three to four flowers on each branch; May–July. Can be bought in winter and spring. Be sure that foliage has not yellowed. Freshness of leaves is a good indication of excellence. Avoid any that have mildewy rot on the stems. Lasts well (10 days) if not shaken or disturbed.

Rhododendron *Rhododendron*
Flowers: white, pink, rose, lilac, rose-purple, often shaded and charmingly freckled; trumpet-shaped; borne in clusters, usually with a rosette of shiny, dark green leaves framing them; May–June. Better used alone with their own leaves as they tend to dominate other flowers. Makes a striking arrangement. Crush stem ends. Spraying with a mist of water helps buds open. Lasts very well.

Rose *Rosa*
Traditionally the Queen of flowers. There are literally thousands of varieties and I advise readers to refer to the many catalogues of rose growers in order to make a choice, particularly for hybrid teas and floribundas, which are continuously becoming fashionable and then often soon disappearing. There are some nurserymen who raise varieties especially suitable for flower arranging. Apart from the more usual teas and flori-bundas, there are several other types of roses that are of especial interest to flower arrangers for various reasons – tinted and autumn-coloured foliage, coloured hips, arching branches, producing flowers outside the usual summer flowering season, e.g. April and May, etc. These include the hybrid perpetuals of the Victorians (still available are Frau Karl Druschki and Mrs John Laing), the species roses, the *albas*, *gallicas*, damasks, cabbage roses, moss roses, china roses (including the bizarre green-flowered form, *R. chinensis* 'Viridiflora'), Bourbons, hybrid musks, *R. rubrifolia* (with plum-tinted, greyish foliage borne on long, wand-like branches), *R. rugosa* and *moyesii* (both of which have beautiful coloured fruits in autumn), and the charming miniature roses which are superb for miniature arrangements. Always cut roses in the cool of morning or evening. Cut semi-double and double roses when in tight bud; very full varieties should be slightly open. Leave 5-leaflet leaves on the stem by cutting ¼ in above first full leaf with a slanting cut with sharp secateurs.
Condition roses: remove leaves and thorns likely to be submerged; cut base of stem with slanting cut. Keep for several hours or over-night in deep water in cool and shelter. Commercial preservatives may be used, but avoid chemicals like aspirin. Avoid copper containers. If heads droop, roll roses in a tube of newspaper to support them until they have drunk water.

S

Salpiglossis *Salpiglossis sinuata*
Ivory, yellow, gold, crimson, violet, blue; July–September. The flowers are short-lived but buds are continuously opening.

Salvia (Blue Sage) *Salvia farinacea*
Lavender-blue; July–August.

Scabiosa (Pincushion Flower) *Scabiosa caucasica*
Soft, light blue, white, mauve and violet blue; June–September. Choose flowers with outer petals just opened and puffy centres.

Scilla (Squill) *Scilla sibirica*
Deep bright blue; March.
S. hispanica, now called *Endymion hispanicus* (Spanish bluebell): lavender blue, white, pink; May. Should be pulled, not cut. Not long-lasting, but cheerful for early miniature arrangements.

Sea Lavender (see Statice)

Shasta Daisy *Chrysanthemum maximum*
White, yellow; 3–6-in single and double daisy-like flowers; June–August. Long-lasting. Scrape skins below waterline. Varieties: 'Esther Reade': white; 'Cobham Gold': creamy yellow.

Snapdragon *Antirrhinum majus*
White, yellow, orange, pink, lavender, crimson; July onwards. Many good varieties, which are listed in current seed catalogues. Long-lasting; useful flowers for arranging. Conditioning: strip off lower foliage; sharp slanting cut at stem end.

Snowdrop *Galanthus*
White, pearl-like; January–March. There are several common snowdrops: Giant, Common, Double, and *Galanthus nivalis* 'S. Arnott' (sweet-scented). Excellent cut flowers, lasting a long time. Charming in nosegays framed with ivy leaves. Conditioning: sharp cut; not too deep water.

Star of Bethlehem *Ornithogalum umbellatum*
White, creamy or green tinged; star-shaped flowers; April–May. *O. narbonense pyramidale*: pyramidal clusters of white with green flowers on 18–24-in stems; July. *O. thyrsoides* (Chincherinchee): white; triangular clusters on 18–24-in stems; May–July. Forced for Christmas. Long-lasting (3–4 weeks). Cut or buy tight buds when colour just shows. Conditioning: sharp cut; remove flowers as they wither; change water regularly.

Statice *Limonium*
Papery-textured flowers which are useful in fresh or dry arrangements. *L. latifolium* (Sea Lavender): lavender; tiny delicate flowers; July–September. *L. sinuata*: white, pink, yellow, lavender, purple; July–September. *L. suworowii* (Rat-tail Statice): lilac; tiny flowers in plumes; July–September.

Stock (Brompton Stock, Stock Gilliflower) *Matthiola incana*
White, cream, pink, rose, lilac, magenta; single or ruffled double rosette flowers; June–July. When buying, see that bottom florets are not papery and that the lower stems are not empty, indicating the cleaning away of withered florets. Conditioning: smash or peel stem below water-line; break or slit end.

Strawflower *Helichrysum bracteatum*
White, yellow, gold, orange, bronze, pink, wine red; double or semi-double; daisy-like centre; shiny bracts; July–September. Cut in bud. Conditioning: remove all lower foliage; change water gradually. Dries well.

Sunflower *Helianthus annuus*
Yellow rays with gold, orange or mahogany centres and/or zones; flowers 5–12 ins across; July–September.

Sweet Pea *Lathyrus odoratus*
White, pink, salmon, scarlet, crimson, lavender, mauve, purple; sometimes with picotee edges; beautiful ruffled pea blossoms borne 3–6 on wiry stems; scented. There are several different types of sweet pea, giving flowers June–September. Sweet peas are not very long-lasting cut flowers. They add charm and scent to mixed arrangements, but personally I think they look best when massed on their own. Conditioning: sharp cut and place into water promptly.

Sweet Sultan *Centaurea moschata*
White, pink, mauve, purple, yellow; long stems; fragrant; July–September. Lasts 1 week–10 days.

Sweet William *Dianthus barbatus*

Purple, red, rose, pink, white, variegated. Large bracted heads. When buying, flowers should have several buds, few withered heads. Conditioning: sharp cut above stem joints.

T

Tansy *Tanacetum vulgare (Chrysanthemum vulgare)*
Yellow-gold; tiny buttons in dense clusters; summer. Conditioning: strip foliage, scrape stems and break ends. Extremely useful as a dry flower.

Tritoma (Red-hot Poker, Torch Lily) *Kniphofia uvaria*
Orange, yellow, red; tubular flowers; June–October. Very dramatic in arrangements.

Trollius (Globe Flower)
Trollius europaeus (Common Globe Flower) and *T. cultorum*
Yellow and orange; May–June. Long-lasting. Cut as bud is opening. Sharp cut; deep water.

Trout Lily (see Erythronium)

Tulip *Tulipa*
Shades of yellow through orange to bronze, white, lavender to purple, sometimes almost black, pale pink to rose to scarlet to crimson, many with stripes, streaks, flecks, edgings, shadings, veinings and even green markings. The basic form of the flowers is a deep cup, but there are numerous subtle variations in shape, size, doubleness and petal structure. They range in height from a few inches to 3 ft. There are over 4,000 varieties. The garden types have been grouped into fifteen divisions according to their various characteristics. Actual varieties of each type can be readily ascertained from growers' catalogues.
T. kaufmanniana: 4–8 ins; March–April.
T. fosteriana: 8–20 ins; April. Large blooms.
T. greigii: 8–12 ins: April. Long-lasting.
T. praestans: 10 ins; April. Flowers often borne in clusters. Cut tulips tight, when buds just showing colour. When buying, tulips should be very crisp and tight, and not flabby or loose with shrinking petal edges. Conditioning: sharp slanting cut at the bottom; support bunches by wrapping in paper and plunge in water until they become stiff and erect. Tulips are light-sensitive in water and tend to get out of position in arrangements. If this happens and they cannot be easily adjusted by cutting and re-arranging, remove from water, allow to become limp and re-condition. Some flop to such an extent that it becomes necessary to wire them. I prefer to do this by twisting the wire round my finger to form a collar to fit under the head of the tulip, rather than piercing the wire straight into the head. Copper containers or copper pennies in the water seem to keep tulips stiff.

V

Verbena *Verbena*
Verbena hybrids, cream, pink,

red, lavender, violet, purple, sometimes with white eyes; tiny flowers in flat, compact clusters 2–3 ins across; sweet-scented. Cut trailing sprays of verbena with buds to soften summer arrangements.

Viburnum *Viburnum*
V. × burkwoodii: pinkish buds and whitish flowers; March–May. *V. carlesii*: pink buds, white flowers; fragrant; April–May. *V. cassinoides* (White Rod): creamy-white; June; pink and blue-black berries; autumn tints. *V. fragrans*: pink and white; very fragrant; November through winter. *V. lantana* (Wayfaring Tree): white flowers; May–June; red to black berries. *V. opulus* (Guelder Rose): white tinged green; June–July; rich autumn tints; scarlet fruits. *V. opulus* 'Sterile' (Snowball Bush): white; globular clusters: June–July. *V. tinus* (Laurustinus); pinkish-white flowers in winter; dark, glossy evergreen foliage. *V. trilobum*, *V. americanum* (Highbush Cranberry): white; July; three-lobed foliage; long-lasting; scarlet berries. Conditioning: crush stem ends.

Viola *Viola × williamsii*
Although close relatives, viola flowers are smaller than pansies. Many colours; May–Autumn. Conditioning: sharp cut and misting with water, if possible.

Violet (Sweet Violet) *Viola odorata*
Violet, rose and white; single and double; February–Autumn; 4–8-in stems; fragrant. Pull rather than cut to obtain long stems. Place in water immediately. Bunches can be bought during winter and early spring. Petals should be smooth and velvety without curled edges. Conditioning: sharp cut; cluster together tightly to minimize evaporation; fine spray with water occasionally.

Virginia Bluebell (Virginia Cowslip) *Mertensia virginica*
Clear, soft blue; bell-shaped flowers with fluted edges clustered along graceful arching branches; May; heavy foliage.

W

Wallflower *Cheiranthus cheiri*
Yellow, orange, red, pink, maroon, purple, brown, white; 1-in flowers clustered on spikes; fragrant; April–June. Cut when bottom flowers on spike have opened. Strip lower foliage. Like many spring flowers, they are not long-lasting, but very pretty.

Wandflower (Harlequin Flower) *Sparaxis*
Cream, yellow, orange, salmon, pink, crimson, lavender; star-shaped flowers (usually with a darker eye) clustered at the tip of a wiry 12–18-in stem; May–June; grass-like foliage. Adds an airy graceful note to mass arrangements.

Waterlily (Lotus) *Nymphaea*
If you can obtain them, they make a beautiful arrangement.

Wisteria *Wisteria sinensis*
Lavender, white; small pea-shaped blossoms in 1-ft long pendant; fragrant; May–June. I offer this hesitantly as a cut flower since I have never found a way to make it last more than two days. However, the flowers on gracefully twisting branches with bronzy new leaves and tendrils arrange so beautifully that it is worth taking a pair of clippers and spending a few minutes every other day to find an interesting new branch.

Witchhazel *Hamamelis mollis*
Golden yellow; strap-petalled flowers clustered like fuzzy balls on bare branches; scented; January–February. Conditioning: hammer stem ends. Branches of witchhazel make airy material for 'spring is coming' arrangements.

Y

Yarrow *Achillea filipendulina*
Yellow, deep gold; tiny flowers in flat, massed plates 3–6 ins across; June–September; fernlike pungent foliage; 3–5-ft stems. An excellent, long-lasting flower for late summer arrangements. Dries exceptionally well.

Z

Zinnia *Zinnia elegans*
Red, orange, yellow, white, pink, salmon, rose, mauve, light green (with some stripes and multi-colours); round heads 1–6 ins in diameter, single to fully double. Wonderful material for summer arrangements. Height 5 ins–3 ft; July–September. They are grouped as follows:
Tall, large-flowered, containing the California Giants, Dahlia, State Fair, Big Tetra, Envy (the green zinnia), Zenith, Ruffled, Jumbo strains.
Medium-sized: Cut-and-Come Again (pumila), Paint Brush, Old Mexico strains.
Small-flowered: Lilliput or pompon, Persian Carpet strains. Dwarf.
Garden-grown zinnias last better in water than bought ones. Cut when flower has just opened. Conditioning: sharp cut above leaf joint; remove lower leaves and excess sprays which may take water from the flowers.

Acknowledgements

The publishers would like to thank the following organizations and individuals for their kind permission to reproduce the pictures in this book:

Bernard Alfieri: endpapers
Barnaby's Picture Library: 36, 80
Robert Brandau: 15, 49, 53, 56 above, 57, 65, 68–69, 73, 84–85, 88, 89, 96
William Danas: 7, 64 above, 64 below
Stella Fennell: 77
Fogg Art Museum, Harvard University, Grenville L. Winthrop bequest: 40
Malcolm Robertson: 29, front and back jacket
Harry Smith Horticultural Photographic Collection: 11, 81
Syndication International: 2–3, 14, 33, 45, 56 below, 61
Ursula Toomey: 24, 25, 72
Werner Wolff, Black Star: 17, 21, 28, 37, 41, 44 above, 44 below, 52 above

Artwork by Hayward Art Group and Vana Haggerty

The author and publishers are most grateful to the Metropolitan Museum of Art in New York for permission to photograph in the American Wing of the Museum. Special credit is due to the following bequests:
(page 49) Architectural element from Powell House, Philadelphia: Rogers Fund, 1925; Table: Rogers Fund; 18th century Chinese wallpaper: Cadwalader Fund, 1914
(pages 68–9) Charger (English, c. 1660–80) and cupboard: gift of Mrs Russell Sage, 1909; Table: gift of Mrs J. Insley Blair, 1949
(page 73) Urn (Vieux Paris Porcelain, c. 1830): gift of Ronald S. Kane, 1968; Table: gift of John Cattus, 1967

The publishers are also very grateful to Kenneth Turner Flowers, London, for permission to use his studio for the photographs on page 29 and the front and back jacket, and for the arrangement on the front jacket.

The arrangement on page 37 and the wreaths and garlanding on page 89 are by William Danas; the arrangement on page 41 is by Giacomo Trotti.

The author and publishers would like to thank the following for their kindness and help on this book: Mrs Edwin T. Bailey, Marilynn Johnson Bordes, William Danas, Mrs Charles Seidler and Mr and Mrs John Wilson.

The author would like to thank C.B.C. for his faith and encouragement, without which this book would neither have been started nor finished.

1. Godetia vinosa — 2. Œnothera striata — 3. Godetia rubicunda — 4. Godetia lepida —
5. Godetia humifusa — 6. Godetia cheiranthifolia — 7. Œnothera tetraptera — 8. Godetia roseo alba —
9. Œnothera Drummondii — 10. Godetia Romanzovii — 11. Œnothera conciana.